MAPPING YOUR BIRTHCHART

About the Author

Stephanie Jean Clement, Ph.D. (Colorado) holds a doctorate in Transpersonal Psychology and has practiced astrology for nearly thirty years. Her other books include *Power of the Midheaven*, *Charting Your Spiritual Path with Astrology*, *What Astrology Can Do For You*, and *Dreams: Working Interactive*.

To Write to the Author

If you wish to contact the author or would like more information about this book, please write to the author in care of Llewellyn Worldwide and we will forward your request. Both the author and publisher appreciate hearing from you and learning of your enjoyment of this book and how it has helped you. Llewellyn Worldwide cannot guarantee that every letter written to the author can be answered, but all will be forwarded. Please write to:

Stephanie Jean Clement
℅ Llewellyn Worldwide
P.O. Box 64383, Dept. 0-7387-0202-1
St. Paul, MN 55164-0383, U.S.A.

Please enclose a self-addressed stamped envelope for reply,
or $1.00 to cover costs. If outside U.S.A., enclose
international postal reply coupon.

Many of Llewellyn's authors have websites with additional information and resources. For more information, please visit our website at
http://www.llewellyn.com

MAPPING YOUR BIRTHCHART

Understanding Your Needs & Potential

STEPHANIE JEAN CLEMENT, Ph.D.

2003
Llewellyn Publications
St. Paul, Minnesota 55164-0383, U.S.A.

First Edition
First Printing, 2003

Book design by Donna Burch
Cover art © 2003 by Digital Stock
Cover design by Kevin R. Brown
Editing by Andrea Neff

Chart wheels were produced by the Kepler program by permission of Cosmic Patterns Software, Inc. (www.AstroSoftware.com)

Library of Congress Cataloging-in-Publication Data

Clement, Stephanie Jean.
    Mapping your birthchart : understanding your needs & potential / Stephanie Jean Clement.—1st ed.
        p.   cm.
    Includes bibliographical references and index.
    ISBN 0-7387-0202-1
        1. Astrology. I. Title.

BF1708.1.C535 2003
133.5—dc21   2003044686

Llewellyn Publications
A Division of Llewellyn Worldwide, Ltd.
P.O. Box 64383, Dept. 0-7387-0202-1
St. Paul, MN 55164-0383, U.S.A.
www.llewellyn.com

Printed in the United States of America

Other Books by Stephanie Jean Clement, Ph.D.

Charting Your Career
(1999)

Dreams: Working Interactive (with Terry Lee Rosen)
(2000)

What Astrology Can Do for You
(2000)

Charting Your Spiritual Path with Astrology
(2001)

Civilization Under Attack (editor and contributor)
(2001)

Power of the Midheaven
(2001)

Meditation for Beginners
(2002)

Meditación para principiantes
(2002)

Forthcoming Books by Stephanie Jean Clement, Ph.D.

Mapping Your Family Relationships
(2004)

Consciousness for Beginners
(2005)

To my teachers, from whom I have learned what I know
of astrology, psychology, and spirituality

To my students, from whom I have learned what it means to be a beginner again

and

To Greg

Contents

List of Charts

All chart data came from AstroDatabank (www.astrodatabank.com).

Acknowledgments

Without Lois Rodden and Mark McDonough, astrologers would lack the largest and most accurate database of birth information in the world. They bring their hearts and minds to their work every day. The charts in this book use data from the AstroDatabank collection (www.astrodatabank.com).

Modern astrological tools for delineation and forecasting are all based on the most accurate calculations possible, to assure the best results of the astrologer's work. The charts and program in this book use a program designed by Cosmic Patterns, an astrology software company in Gainesville, Florida. David and Fei Cochrane have been unceasing in their support for this book and CD-ROM program.

Without the Mind of the Universe—God and Goddess—who designed an elegant, resourceful, and dynamic world for us, we would be nothing. This is the root source of my inspiration.

Introduction

Why Learn Astrology?

Instead of writing a long, boring statement of why I think astrology is important, and why I think you should study the subject, I have decided to make a list of questions that can be answered by examining your birthchart. If you have asked some of these questions, you are the reader I had in mind when I was writing this book.

- What is astrology?
- Why is my birth time so important?
- What do all those symbols on my chart mean?
- How do I create a chart? Do I have to learn a lot of math?
- What does this computer program do?
- Can I forecast the future?
- What are astrological houses? Are they different from the signs?
- What about the empty spaces in my chart?
- Is my chart really bad? Really good?
- Does my chart determine my life?

- It's too complicated. Can't you just give me a printout?
- What about relationships? Career? Family?

Astrology provides a map for your entire life. It tells about the potential you were born with, and it provides a lot of ideas for what to do with that potential. It helps you understand how different areas of your life fit together. It can show difficult areas, and ways to resolve problems. It can also indicate possibilities that you have never considered.

No single subject has held my attention as long as astrology. I have had several careers, but astrology is the one thing I continue to study and practice. It has helped me understand my family, my own life, and the world. I don't look at my chart every day, or even every week. Still, after thirty years, astrology provides insights that are not readily available from any other source.

In studying astrology, you will learn why you and your friends seem unique, and yet are so alike. You will understand why your parents' generation is so different from your own. The map you find in astrology is just that—a map. Remember, the map is not the territory. You get to decide where to apply your time and energy. Astrology is here to show you the possibilities!

1
The Basics of Astrology

Let's begin by looking at an astrological chart (chart 1). This chart was produced by the CD-ROM program included with this book. The program performs all the mathematical calculations, based on the birth date, time, and place. The result is a two-dimensional "map" of where all the planets were in the zodiac at the time for which the chart was created. In order to make this more real, I have used the chart of a real person—George W. Bush—as an illustration.

Notice that part of this chart is full of notations, while several of the sections of the circle are empty. Each chart you look at will have a different arrangement of information. Empty sections simply indicate areas of life that are less dominant or interesting to the individual, while occupied sections show where the person's attention is likely to go. There are many components in the chart, and I will introduce them in this chapter.

Can't wait to create your own chart? Turn to appendix 2 for instructions on how to use the enclosed CD-ROM program, which includes step-by-step directions on how to re-create George W. Bush's chart. Just insert the data for your own birth date, time, and place.

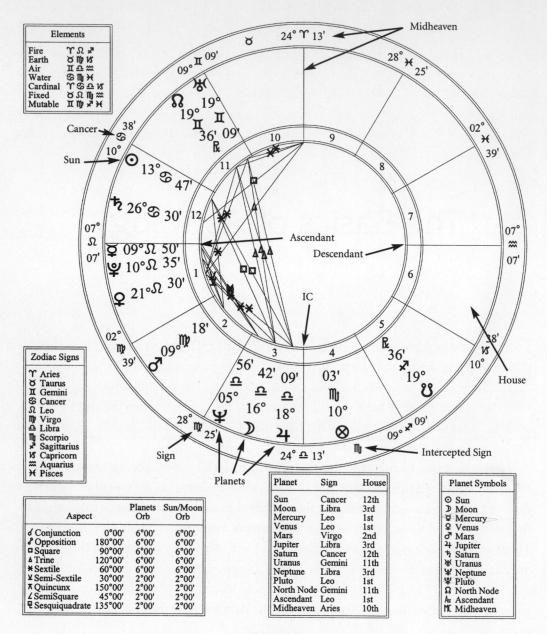

Elements	
Fire	♈ ♌ ♐
Earth	♉ ♍ ♑
Air	♊ ♎ ♒
Water	♋ ♏ ♓
Cardinal	♈ ♋ ♎ ♑
Fixed	♉ ♌ ♏ ♒
Mutable	♊ ♍ ♐ ♓

Zodiac Signs	
♈	Aries
♉	Taurus
♊	Gemini
♋	Cancer
♌	Leo
♍	Virgo
♎	Libra
♏	Scorpio
♐	Sagittarius
♑	Capricorn
♒	Aquarius
♓	Pisces

Aspect		Planets Orb	Sun/Moon Orb
☌	Conjunction	0°00'	6°00'	6°00'
☍	Opposition	180°00'	6°00'	6°00'
□	Square	90°00'	6°00'	6°00'
△	Trine	120°00'	6°00'	6°00'
✶	Sextile	60°00'	6°00'	6°00'
⚺	Semi-Sextile	30°00'	2°00'	2°00'
⚻	Quincunx	150°00'	2°00'	2°00'
∠	SemiSquare	45°00'	2°00'	2°00'
⚼	Sesquiquadrate	135°00'	2°00'	2°00'

Planet	Sign	House
Sun	Cancer	12th
Moon	Libra	3rd
Mercury	Leo	1st
Venus	Leo	1st
Mars	Virgo	2nd
Jupiter	Libra	3rd
Saturn	Cancer	12th
Uranus	Gemini	11th
Neptune	Libra	3rd
Pluto	Leo	1st
North Node	Gemini	11th
Ascendant	Leo	1st
Midheaven	Aries	10th

Planet Symbols	
☉	Sun
☽	Moon
☿	Mercury
♀	Venus
♂	Mars
♃	Jupiter
♄	Saturn
♅	Uranus
♆	Neptune
♇	Pluto
☊	North Node
Aꜱ	Ascendant
ℳℂ	Midheaven

Chart 1
George W. Bush, Birthchart

July 6, 1946 / New Haven, CT / 7:26 A.M. EST

Koch Houses

Chart Components

The main parts of the astrological chart are the signs, planets, houses, and aspects. These are arranged in the circle. The lines in the center of the circle connect points that are in aspect to each other. The symbols on each line indicate the aspect involved. The planets signify who or what is active in our lives, the signs tell how the planet is acting, and the houses tell us where in life the action takes place. The relationships between the planets are the aspects.

Signs

Let's take the signs first. On the left side of the chart form, there is a list of names and glyphs (symbols) for each sign. Each sign represents a particular psychological need, reflected in certain tendencies within the personality.

Sign	Symbol	Need
Aries	♈	To be self-confident and free; to lead
Taurus	♉	To be resourceful and productive
Gemini	♊	To communicate
Cancer	♋	To give and receive emotional warmth and security
Leo	♌	To create and express oneself
Virgo	♍	To analyze and find order
Libra	♎	To create harmony and balance
Scorpio	♏	To experience intense emotional transformation
Sagittarius	♐	To explore and expand horizons
Capricorn	♑	To find structure and social acknowledgment
Aquarius	♒	To innovate, be original, and break forms
Pisces	♓	To gain faith and belief in transcendence

Everyone has all twelve signs in their chart, and therefore everyone's chart reflects these needs somewhere in their lives. When you talk about your own sign, you are referring to the place where the Sun is. George W. Bush has the Sun in the sign of Cancer. Usually you only need the birth date to determine the Sun sign. For the day when the Sun changes signs, you need to know the time as well.

Houses

The second factor is the houses. There are also twelve of them. The numbers around the center circle of the chart indicate which house is which. The First House is always just below the horizon (the horizontal line on the left side of the circle). There are signs on both cusps (edges) of each house, and sometimes there is a whole sign inside the house. In George W. Bush's chart you can see symbols for Taurus (♉) in the middle of House 10 and for Scorpio (♏) in the middle of House 4. This means that these whole signs are found inside the Tenth and Fourth Houses. Astrologers call them intercepted signs.

The cusp of the house is the first edge, going in a counterclockwise direction. The houses represent the different activities and experiences we encounter throughout our lives (chart 2).

House	Experience
1	Physical body, persona
2	Money and other personal resources
3	Education, neighborhood, siblings
4	Parents, family, home
5	Children and creativity
6	Health, work environment
7	Partnerships of all kinds, including romantic relationships
8	Sex, death, other people's resources
9	Religion, travel, philosophy
10	Career, social standing
11	Friends, groups of associates, circumstances beyond your personal control
12	Private affairs, secrets, institutions

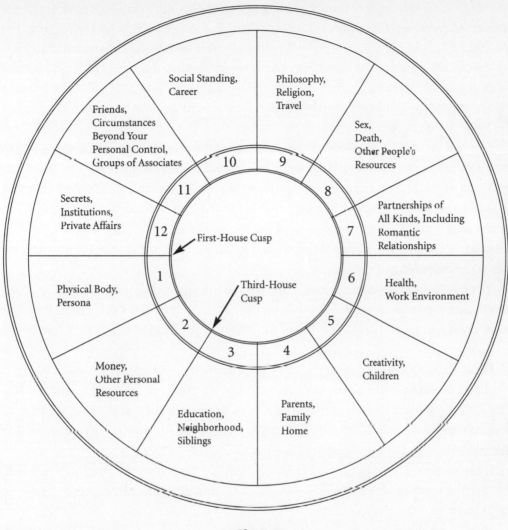

Chart 2
The Houses

The Sun only moves a little way through the zodiac—about 1 degree—each day. Yet it appears to travel across the sky as the Earth turns. For example, at noon the Sun is in the Midheaven—it is at its highest point in the sky, and is therefore at the top of the chart. At about 6:00 A.M. the Sun is in the Ascendant—the point in the east where it rises. At around 6:00 P.M. the Sun is at the Seventh House, and at midnight it is at the Fourth-House cusp at the bottom of the chart wheel. The time of day you were born determines the position of the Sun in the chart.

The time of day you were born also determines the arrangement of the signs within the houses. The twelve signs of the zodiac rise and set during each twenty-four-hour period, just as the Sun does. Each sign moves across the Midheaven, or middle of the sky, in about two hours, and a different sign rises in the east (left part of the chart). The Midheaven is at the top of the chart, and the Ascendant, or rising sign, is on the left side at the horizon line. The signs are shown in the outside ring, at the lines (cusps) that indicate the beginning of each house.

The Sun rises at dawn in the east, at the Ascendant, and is on the Descendant at about sunset. The Midheaven is the noon point in the chart. If the Sun is there in a chart, the birth time is close to noon. The *Imum Coeli* (sometimes called the Nadir) represents midnight and is opposite the Midheaven.

By locating the Sun in the wheel, you can estimate the time of birth. George W. Bush was born at 7:26 A.M. in the summer, so we know the Sun rose earlier that day. His Sun (☉) is in the Twelfth House. The signs rise in a clockwise motion at the rate of about 15 degrees each hour, and the Sun is about 24 degrees above the horizon, so we know that the Sun rose about one and one-half hours or so before he was born. This seems about right for someone born in July in the United States. This is one way you can verify that the chart is approximately correct—the Sun (☉) appears where you expect to find it in the twenty-four-hour wheel of the chart, based on the birth time.

What does the sign on each house tell us? The sign represents a psychological need, and the house represents an area of your life. When you combine the sign and house, you discover how you work out your needs—what people or activities you expect will help or hinder you in fulfilling your needs. Everyone has the same needs, but we express these needs in very individual ways, based upon where the signs are located in the houses. This is a profound truth to be explored through astrology. If you never do anything else with astrology, understanding your own needs in terms of the signs and houses will be a powerful tool in your life. The same holds true for your family and friends. If you understand their needs more clearly, you will be able to help them and have compassion for them.

The Sun sign is what people mean when they ask, "What's your sign?" George W. Bush is a Cancer—he has the Sun (☉) in the sign of Cancer (♋) in the Twelfth House of his birthchart. By looking at the tables in this chapter for basic planet, sign, and house meanings, we find that his psychological need as an individual is to give and receive emotional warmth and security (Cancer ♋), and the area where this need is expressed is his private or secret life (Twelfth House).

What does this mean? We can anticipate that Mr. Bush will not express his feelings in public very much because that is a private thing for him. He will not seek to give and receive emotional warmth, as he takes care of that need in private. What do we see? Mr. Bush is a rather formal person who maintains proper, even ceremonial, behavior in public. He dresses for the occasion—he can appear in jeans and a plaid shirt for less formal events but looks quite comfortable in suits when a more reserved look is required. He does not display his feelings openly.

Looking at my own chart, I have the Sun (☉) in Scorpio (♏) in the Seventh House. I (the Sun ☉) need intense, emotionally transformative experiences (Scorpio ♏) in my relationships (Seventh House). No dull friendships and marriages for me in this lifetime! I work with partners of all kinds to inspire transformation in myself. These changes are emotional and sometimes embarrassingly public. What a contrast with Mr. Bush, whose most immediate emotional needs are satisfied in private.

Planets

The Sun, Moon, and planets represent the parts of our being. They also indicate people who come into our lives—people who have the characteristics of the planet and the sign where the planet is found. The symbols and names of the planets are listed at the lower right part of the chart form. The house placements of each planet are listed at the bottom center of the form. Chart 3 shows the rulership associations of the planets and signs. The following table includes the symbols for the planets and a few words about the part of the personality that each planet reflects.

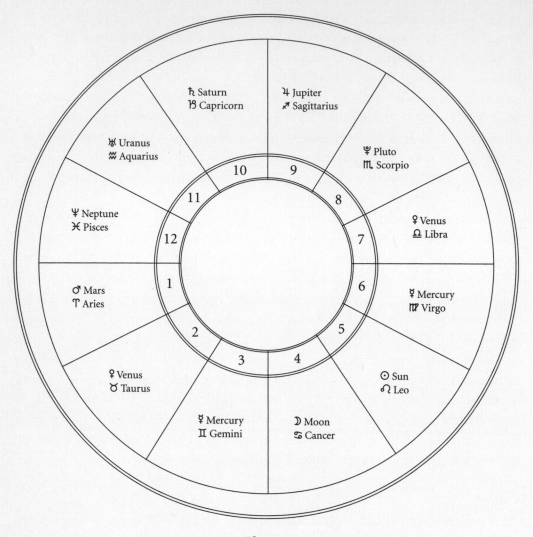

Chart 3
Rulership Associations of the Planets and Signs

Planet	Associated Sign(s)	Part of the Personality	People or Things in the Environment
☉ Sun	♌ Leo	Expression, individuality	Men, leaders, daytime
☽ Moon	♋ Cancer	Feelings and habits	Women, nighttime, the masses
☿ Mercury	♊ Gemini, ♍ Virgo	Communication style	Students or teachers
♀ Venus	♉ Taurus, ♎ Libra	Value system, social attraction	Women, beautiful things
♂ Mars	♈ Aries	Desire and action, energy	Men, sharp things
♃ Jupiter	♐ Sagittarius	The process of expansion	Religious or legal people; big things
♄ Saturn	♑ Capricorn	Structure, responsibility	Police, cautious people, detailed things
♅ Uranus	♒ Aquarius	Intuition, ritual, sudden change	Unusual people, anything new
♆ Neptune	♓ Pisces	Receptivity, imagination	Sensitive people, strange things
♇ Pluto	♏ Scorpio	Power and will	Forceful people, organizations
ASC Ascendant		Persona, physical body	
MC Midheaven		Self-awareness, achievement	

Aspects

The fourth factor in chart interpretation is the aspect—the distance between the planets in a particular chart. Certain harmonic relationships—divisions of the 360 degree circle by whole numbers—have been found to be significant in charts. Some astrologers consider a wide range of aspects and others stick to a few. Chart 4 shows the aspects in a chart wheel. The following table lists the most commonly used aspects.

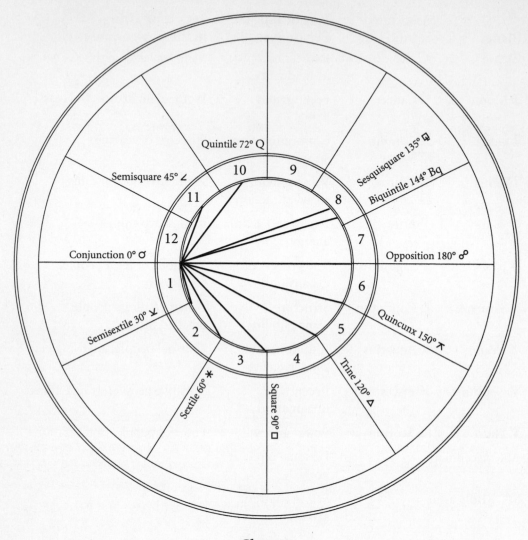

Chart 4
Aspects

Aspect	Symbol	Harmonic	Exact Number of Degrees	Meaning	Orb Allowed
Conjunction	☌	360	0	Beginning and ending	6
Opposition	☍	2	180	Awareness	6
Trine	△	3	120	Comfort	6
Square	□	4	90	Challenge	6
Sextile	✳	6	60	Opportunity	6
Quintile	Q	5	72	Talent and creativity	3
Septile	⑦	7	51.2	Fate	2
Semisquare	∠	8	45	Tension	2
Semisextile	⌄	12	30	Growth	2
Biquintile	Bq	5	144	Creativity	3
Sesquisquare	⍁	8	135	Agitation	2
Quincunx	⊼	12	150	Adjustment	2

The chart itself contains 360 degrees. The conjunction aspect occurs when two planets are exactly together. Mr. Bush has Mercury (☿) very close to Pluto (♇) in his chart, so they are said to be conjunct. The same is true for the Moon (☽) and Jupiter (♃), even though they are about 1½ degrees apart. Each planet has an orb of influence—the planets only need to be within the number of degrees of orb to be forming an aspect. You can relate this idea of an orb to tuning a radio station. You don't have to be right on the exact spot on the dial to receive the signal. The closer you are to the exact signal, the more easily you can hear the message. I recommend orbs of 6 degrees or less when looking at the birthchart, and only 1 degree when considering transits.

In our example, Mr. Bush has Mercury (☿) and Pluto (♇) close together in the First House in Leo. They are within 1 degree of the exact conjunction. His need to be creative and to express himself (Leo ♌) is centered in the physical body and persona (First

House). His communication style (Mercury ☿) and his power and will (Pluto ♇) are closely associated (conjunction ☌) in fulfilling this need. Does this make sense when we look at the president and his political actions? Realistically, we can speculate about his life, but we are limited by what the media tell us about him, and generally we see him in his political role. However, we can say that Mr. Bush creates for himself a persona of power, will, and communication. He uses his physical body and persona to project these traits. He surrounds himself with people who either have these traits, help him possess and project these traits, or both. His success in this area depends on other aspects in his chart and his own will—he works to overcome apparent limitations and to maximize natural advantages.

Transits

Another factor in astrology is transits—the positions of the planets on any given day. The transits can be thought of as a river of energy flowing through time. A transit chart is simply a natal chart for a specific time and place. Your birthchart is a transit chart for your birth time. By comparing the planetary positions now to those in your birthchart, you can understand where you are in the "currents" of planetary energy, and how those currents affect your life.

Chart 5 combines George W. Bush's birthchart with the transits for December 18, 2000, by matching up the signs. The inner chart is the same as his birthchart, and the outer circle contains the positions of the planets for December 18, 2000, the day when Mr. Bush knew for certain that he had been elected president. On that day the transiting Moon (☽) made an exact sextile (✳) to his Mercury (☿), and transiting Pluto (♇) made a quincunx aspect (⚻) to his Sun (☉).

By using the simple keywords presented in this chapter, we can conclude that the general feelings of the day (Moon ☽) were aligned with Mr. Bush's communication style (Mercury ☿) to provide an opportunity (sextile ✳). The power and will of the day (Pluto ♇) reflected an adjustment (quincunx ⚻) in his expression (Sun ☉) of feelings (in Cancer ♋) in private (Twelfth House). We all know that he will have to give up a great deal of privacy in his role as president, but we can conclude from these aspects that the necessary adjustments are not going to be all bad, as he is no doubt happy about the opportunity that came his way as a result of the election.

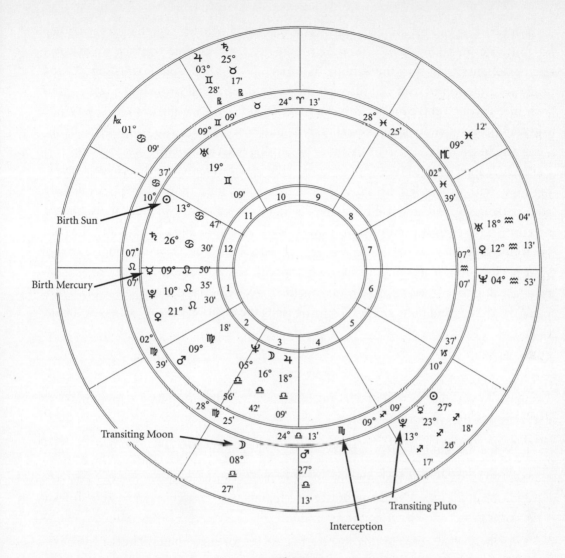

Chart 5

George W. Bush Transit Chart

Inner Wheel	*Outer Wheel*
George W. Bush, Birthchart	George W. Bush, Transit Chart
July 6, 1946 / New Haven, CT	December 18, 2000 / Washington, D.C.
7:26 A.M. EST	5:00 P.M. EST
Koch Houses	Koch Houses

When the aspects between the transit chart and the birthchart agree with each other, we find smooth sailing. Where they are in disagreement, or even conflict, we discover the personality traits and the actions that make people uniquely interesting. As you study your own chart, you will discover the smooth spots and the rough edges in your own life. Through this process, you can make friends with yourself in a new way, and you can incorporate prickly personality traits more successfully into your overall being. Then you begin to satisfy needs that may be causing you difficulty or unhappiness.

Each chapter of this book will expand on the ideas presented in this chapter, showing how each planet, sign, house, and aspect reveals details about your physical body, your personality, and how you travel life's path. I have related the planets, signs, houses, and aspects by their common expressions—Mars, Aries, the First House, and the conjunction aspect all share certain energetic expressions, each portrayed through a part of your personality, an area of your life, and a specific focus of energy. This book is organized around the planets and their "personalities." As we proceed, I will also explain how you can foresee conditions in your future by using the positions of the planets in the sky each day.

Exercise

Using your own chart or that of a friend, look at each symbol. You may want to make an extra copy of the chart for this exercise.

1. Write the name of each sign next to its symbol in the chart.
2. Write the name of each planet next to its symbol.
3. Look at the aspect grid and notice which planets are closely associated with each other.
4. Using the keywords in this chapter, make a list for each planet. The list will have the words for the planet first, then the words for the sign, and then the words for the house.
5. Now, using some of these words, make up sentences that describe the energy, as I did with George W. Bush's chart.
6. Notice how these sentences fit what you know about yourself or your friend.
7. Adjust the sentences by using different words.

When you have finished, you have your first, very basic chart delineation! You can see how easily ideas come together in words to describe yourself astrologically.

Summary

In the following chapters, we will explore each planet, sign, house, and aspect in greater detail. You may find it helpful to memorize the keywords in this chapter so that you have a basic concept for each part of the astrological chart. You will also want to learn to recognize the symbols for the planets, signs, and aspects quickly and easily. Then you will begin to "read" the chart directly.

2
The Zodiac

In the introduction, you read the most basic information about the signs of the zodiac from the astrological perspective. Now we will look at the zodiac itself, and each sign, in greater depth.

What Is the Zodiac?

The night sky is filled with stars that have been arranged into figures. Not all cultures depict the same figures, yet the constellations are remarkably similar across cultures.

Constellations

The constellations are the actual depictions of mythological and other characters in the sky. In the Northern Hemisphere most of them are figures from ancient mythology. Astronomers have separated them with defined lines, so that the stars in each area can be labeled by the name of the constellations without ambiguity. Twelve of these constellations have the same names as the signs of the zodiac. These twelve are found along the ecliptic—the apparent path of the Sun through the sky (which is the actual path of the Earth around the Sun). The other constellations are only occasionally mentioned in astrology.

Tropical Zodiac

The 360 degree zodiac is a band of celestial space on either side of the ecliptic, and it is divided into twelve equal 30 degree spaces. The constellations are not uniform in size, but the signs are. Tropical astrology is the astrology used by most Western astrologers. In this system, the beginning of Aries, the first sign of the zodiac, is defined as the beginning of spring. It is the time when the Sun begins its travel north of the equator.

There was a time about 4,000 years ago when the first day of spring also coincided with the early part of the constellation Aries, but that is no longer so. The spring equinox moves backward through the heavens, due to the slight shift of the Earth's axis. It takes about 2,000 years for the equinox point to move one full sign. The symbol for Pisces, the two fishes, is strongly associated with Christianity, which developed during the Age of Pisces. When we talk of the Age of Aquarius, we refer to the fact that the equinox is now occurring in the constellation of Aquarius.

In using the equinox as our starting point, we focus on the growth cycle as it is experienced in the Northern Hemisphere. The signs are related to the stages of growth through the year, including the death and dormancy period of late fall and early winter. This cycle will be included in explanations of each sign.

Mythology of Each Sign

The mythological characters represented by the zodiac signs have stories that reflect the general meaning of each sign.[1] These characters embody the qualities of each sign.

Aries

 The symbol for Aries is the ram. The equinox occurred in the sign of the ram at about the time the myth of the golden fleece developed, and there are earlier stories about infants who escaped the wrath of Zeus on the back of a ram with gold fleece. However, the Greek god Ares (Roman god Mars) is often depicted as the god of war. He is the mythological figure who inspires courage in his devotees, and panic or terror in his enemies. Mars is also an agricultural god.

Both depictions, the warlike god and the agricultural god, make sense when we think of Aries as the first sign in the spring. The warrior Ares is assertive, even aggressive, and this is the quality of plants as they push their way up through the soil from seeds. Ares and Aphrodite (Roman Venus) are intimate partners in mythology, and the sign Taurus, often associated with Venus, follows Aries in the zodiac.

Taurus

The bull turns up in several mythologies. The Greek god Zeus took the form of a bull to pursue Europa. She was taken to Crete, and her path is the historical path of civilization, moving from the Middle East into Europe (her namesake). In the Vedas of India, Mitras (who became Mithras in Roman cults) was a bringer of light. Mithras is said to have conquered and slain the bull. In death, the bull's body sprouted all the useful plants found throughout the world, and its blood became the wine used in religious services.

The bull can also be peaceful, wandering about in a field, soaking up the sunshine. This period of the year finds plants reaching into the sunshine and growing toward the Sun, which is not so high in the sky yet, and therefore not too hot for tender young shoots. The planet Venus is associated with Taurus.

Gemini

The theme of twins runs throughout literature. There are the Greek twins Castor and Polydeuces (Pollox), the Roman twins Romulus and Remus, and also later stories in Greek, English, and Spanish literature about the confused identity of twins. Castor and Pollox were born from an egg—their mother was Leda, and Zeus, in the form of a swan, was their father. These twins, one mortal and one immortal, share a place together in the heavens that they could not share on Earth after Castor died.

Gemini signals the calm weather characteristic of late spring. Plants are spreading their leaves and blossoms, animal life is becoming visible and vigorous, and birds complete their migration northward to begin a new nesting cycle. The planet Mercury, known for the capacity to move about freely, is associated with this sign.

Cancer

The crab, depicted as a scarab beetle by the Egyptians, is an enigmatic symbol. The crab is mute, so communication must occur through other means. The Moon is associated with this sign, and lunar mythology is easier to trace than mythology of the crab. Mother goddesses in various cultures are related to the Moon. These goddesses embody the wealth of maternal feelings, both in begetting and in caring for offspring.

During the season following the summer solstice, the world seems totally involved with the raising of a new generation of birds, mammals, and other wildlife. Frogs fill wetlands with their croaky voices, and young animals can be seen in their nests or with their mothers, even in urban environments. Yet at the same time the Sun has ceased to climb in the sky, and now moves sideways and downward toward its lowest winter point. This movement is reminiscent of the crab's own style of movement.

Leo

The lion has a rich mythology in Egypt, Babylon, and India. The Egyptian goddess Bast was originally a lion and later depicted with the head of a cat. She is related to the sun god Ra (her father/brother/spouse). The massive stone lion of Babylon tramples a man beneath his feet. The lion is among the many avatars of Vishnu, a solar deity. Thus the relationship between Leo, the lion, and the Sun is well established around the world. In Greek myth the first labor of Hercules was to strangle the Nemean lion.

The Sun is in the zodiac sign of Leo when the summer heat is the strongest. Fruit is ripening and vegetables are developing in anticipation of the first harvest. The creative urge is very strong at this time, and it is a good time for human pregnancy, as the birth will then be expected in the spring, after the ravages of winter are past.

Virgo

The sign Virgo is associated with the end of summer. In Assyro-Babylonian myth, Ishtar, goddess of the harvest, entered the underworld to save her lover Tammuz, thus causing desolation on the Earth in the form of winter. The gods rescued her (and thus Tammuz) and brought her back to life. The Greek Demeter (Roman Ceres) is the goddess of the field. In a very similar tale, Demeter's sorrow (this time over the loss of her daughter) caused the gods to intervene. It was decided that Kore (Persephone) would live with her mother for most of the year, but would have to return to the underworld for one-third of the year to live with her husband, Hades. In this way the seasons were established.

Virgo signals the harvesting of corn and ripe fruit. The energy of this sign reflects the diligence of the farmer in planting and caring for the crop, as well as the celebration of the harvest. The focus of this sign is on teamwork and behavior that is appropriate to the task at hand.

Libra

The Egyptian Maat, the deity responsible for truth and justice, was said to weigh the heart of the deceased person to measure its purity. In Greek mythology Themis turns up again and again in similar roles. She was one of the twelve Titans, and it was her role to regulate moral and physical order in the world. Her children included the seasons, legislation, justice (Dike), and the Fates. She protected the just and punished the wicked. Both Maat and Themis held the scales and thus represented balance.

The sign of Libra occurs at the autumn equinox, when the Sun moves from north declination to south at the beginning of the fall season. There is a sense of balance at this time of the year, when the harvest is gathered and people offer thanks. The social aspect of this sign is seen in community and partnerships of all kinds.

Scorpio

The scorpion was said to be responsible for the death of Orion, the hunter. These two constellations occupy opposite parts of the sky, and they pursue each other through the seasons. The Egyptian Selket, one of the protectors of the dead, is sometimes portrayed as part human, part scorpion. Her role was to preserve the entrails of the embalmed, pending future rebirth. The sexual power associated with this sign is reflected in Ishtar, who, unlike Selket the protectress, killed her many consorts. Thus the sign of Scorpio has a mixed mythology of sex, death, and transformation.

The sign Scorpio occupies the part of the year when the frost comes to kill plant life. It represents the struggle for survival that begins with the onset of cold weather. Anything that cannot protect itself dies, but the seeds that have been produced endure to sprout and grow again, thus reflecting the transformative quality of this sign.

Sagittarius

The story of this sign focuses on the centaur Chiron, who was shot by a poisoned arrow from Hercules' bow. His wound would not heal, and he eventually took his place in the heavens in the sign of Sagittarius (some say Chiron is actually seen in the southern constellation of the Centaur). Before this fate, Chiron tutored Achilles, a child who was born due to Chiron's advice to Peleus. Of course, Achilles also had a fatal vulnerability, in spite of his mother's attempts to protect him from his pronounced fate.

The sign Sagittarius is associated with the philosophical wisdom of Chiron. Deep in the period of the Sun's darkest season, this sign provides for meditation and religious activity, seen in the fires of the winter solstice that are lit to encourage the return of the Sun. Sagittarius reflects the spiritual side of life and also the sense of dreaming and the hope of the renewal of spring.

Capricorn

The mythology of Capricorn is often confused with the god Pan, who is part human, part goat. Capricorn is usually depicted as part fish, part goat. The symbolism of this sign is perhaps the most obscure. The dual nature of the sign suggests that people born at this time have the capacity to live on land (as conscious beings), but also to survive in the water (the arena of the unconscious mind). Some sources say that the god Pan, in order to escape from Typhon, jumped into the river. The lower part of his body became a fish, while the upper part remained a goat.[2]

Capricorn is the sign that begins the winter cycle. Even though the intense cold of winter is focused in this sign, as the Sun begins its return to the Northern Hemisphere, the invisible return of life to the plant kingdom begins with sap running in trees. A similar energy shift occurs for people—preparation for the spring starts here, and post-holiday plans for the future are made. Capricorn is the sign of vocation, focused goals, and a seriousness that reflects the struggles of winter.

Aquarius

Aquarius, the water bearer, is generally agreed to represent Ganymede, a mortal youth who was kidnapped by Zeus and taken to Mount Olympus, where he became Zeus' favorite. He can be compared to Soma, a Vedic god whose name is the same as the plant that produces the golden nectar of the gods. Like Ganymede, Soma provides a link between humanity and heaven. Ganymede is one of Jupiter's moons and is larger than the planet Mercury.

Aquarius has a broad perspective, considering many things before making a decision. During this time of the year hopes for the renewal of the year are strong, but it is not yet time to cultivate the earth and plant new crops. Everything is ready, though, so that you can take action at the right moment. Intuition is strong, and there is a good understanding of human nature.

Pisces

 The fish is an ancient symbol of divinity. Matsya, the fish avatar of Vishnu, was nurtured by Manu, a wise man, and later saved Manu from a great flood, along with all the animals. The fish is an early Christian symbol for Jesus and the new religion.

While the Sun is in Pisces, seeds begin to expand and sprout, due to the rains associated with the sign (and the month of March). This sign exemplifies the receptivity of the earth to the rain, as it is the most sympathetic of the signs. The reserve of this sign incorporates receptivity and patience appropriate to the early planting season.

Alchemical Correlations to the Zodiac

Alchemists in both European and Asian cultures associate the matter of the universe with four basic elements: fire, earth, air, and water. Astrologers have also identified three fundamental modes of expression: cardinal, fixed, and mutable. The twelve zodiac signs each reflect one combination of an element and a mode of expression. The elements of fire, earth, air, and water can be likened to the Jungian personality types of intuition, sensation, thinking, and feeling—four ways of expressing oneself in the world. The modes are three styles of expression, called cardinal (directed activity), fixed (sustaining activity), and mutable (changeable activity). We can understand the nature of each sign by examining these energetic combinations.

	Fire	Earth	Air	Water
Cardinal	Aries	Capricorn	Libra	Cancer
Fixed	Leo	Taurus	Aquarius	Scorpio
Mutable	Sagittarius	Virgo	Gemini	Pisces

These simple statements represent core meanings for each of the zodiac signs.

- **Aries** relates to initiating activity
- **Taurus** relates to sustained practical effort

- **Gemini** relates to flexible logic
- **Cancer** relates to an active emotional life
- **Leo** relates to inspirational leadership
- **Virgo** relates to methodical behavior
- **Libra** relates to an active mental process
- **Scorpio** relates to depth of feeling
- **Sagittarius** relates to flexible planning
- **Capricorn** relates to active physical involvement
- **Aquarius** relates to scientific thinking
- **Pisces** relates to empathy and mystical sensitivity

Signs, Planets, and Houses Together

Astrologers associate the signs, planets, and houses in a specific way. Aries is associated with the First House, Taurus with the Second House, and so forth around the chart wheel. Each sign is closely associated with a planet that is said to "rule" the sign. Chart 3 in chapter 1 shows the signs and planets in the appropriate houses.

Exercise

Using a blank sheet of paper, trace the chart wheel shown on the following page, or draw a circle and divide it into twelve houses.

1. Number the houses, starting on the left below the horizontal line, and moving counterclockwise around the chart.
2. Draw the symbols for each sign in the houses, starting with Aries in the First House. Label the symbols with the name for each sign.
3. Draw the planet associated with each sign in the house where the sign is found. Label the planets.

Your chart now has all the symbols (glyphs) for the signs and planets. You can use this one sheet of paper to help you learn the glyphs, and also to memorize which signs and planets are closely associated with each of the houses.

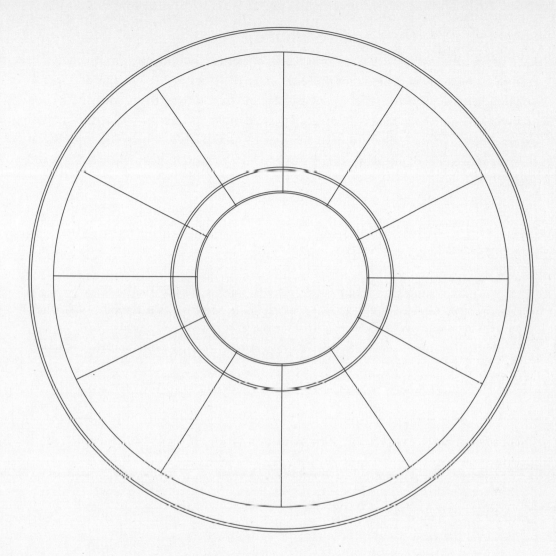

Summary

Each of the next chapters examines one planet, one or two houses, and an aspect. As you read each chapter, you can look for those factors in the chart(s) you are considering. You will build an overall picture of the person(s) behind the chart(s). By the end of the book you will have a very good idea of how each person thinks and acts, as well as the kinds of experiences he or she is likely to have. Chapter 14 on transits will help you understand how the movement of the planets affects us and how you can forecast likely feelings and events.

1. While many of these myths are common knowledge, the reader may want to pursue the subject further. *The New Larousse Encyclopedia of Mythology* is a good source of information about the deities mentioned here. *Beyond the Blue Horizon*, by E. C. Krupp, has information about the zodiacal myths as well. A third source of information on the zodiacal signs is *Archetypes of the Zodiac*, by Kathleen Burt.

2. Elbert Benjamine, "News from the Summerland," bound in C. C. Zain, *Spiritual Astrology* (Los Angeles: The Church of Light, 1960).

3
The Sun, the Fifth House, and the Conjunction

The signs of the zodiac are the background or the stage upon which the planets act out their unique roles. The drama is the interaction among the planets, as seen through the aspects. In this chapter we are looking at the Sun as it occupies each sign. We will also consider the Fifth House, the natural home of the Sun, as well as the conjunction aspect. In later chapters we will consider each of the planets in the different signs.

The Sun

First and foremost, the Sun and its sign reflect the individuality of each person. This is the core human expression that each of us is born with, and often we are able to identify other people's Sun signs. This is especially true of children, who have not learned how to conceal their basic nature. The Sun shows where we feel the urge to express ourselves. It says a lot about how we usually make decisions and how we exert our willpower.

The Sun sign also is an indicator of our general health. Sometimes it points to a weak part of the body, for example, or to a condition that can lead to illness if not cared for properly. The Sun is associated with the heart—both the physical heart and the emotional center. The Sun itself is associated with the father, with leaders, or with other authority figures, and it shows how we can demonstrate authority in our lives.

Finally, in the branch of astrology called mundane astrology, the Sun reflects the nature of the person or event being considered. There are two main kinds of mundane charts. *Horary* astrologers answer questions by preparing a chart for the time (*hora*, or hour) the question is asked. *Mundane* astrologers set up a chart for the time of a specific event. One set of such events, called ingresses, is the movement of the Sun into the cardinal signs—the equinoxes and solstices. Charts can also be prepared for the "birth" of corporations, the start of sporting events, and for other events.

While we normally associate astrology with people's birth dates, astrology is used for other purposes. You may want to keep this in mind as you read each chapter of this book. Each planet has a role in the different kinds of charts, yet the basic nature of the planets and the signs does not change—only the circumstances of the chart change.

The Sun Through the Signs

Sun in Aries

The essence of the fire element is intuition. The essence of the cardinal mode is action. Thus Aries exemplifies action, based upon intuition. Even if you don't realize it, intuition is a strong force in your life if you have the Sun (or other planets) in Aries. You love having a direction in which to go, just like the ram, the symbol of Aries. You do sometimes look at your opposition, put your head down, and charge. If you engage, great. If not, you look around, find another objective, and charge forward again.

As you gain experience in the world, you learn some finesse. Perhaps you consider your choices more carefully before moving ahead. Or maybe you make sure you are in the power position before you take action. Whichever way you go, you are bold and passionate. For you the adage "Haste makes waste" was written to be understood, then ignored.

Sun in Taurus

The essence of the earth element is sensation. The essence of the fixed mode is stability. Thus Taurus exemplifies a solid awareness of the world around you. Your spirit need not be mired in the mud of physical existence, though. You have a rich inner life because you understand the importance of comfort. While Aries approaches things with passion, you persevere to achieve your goals. Money is meaningful to you.

You are a material being, but you are not stuck in a material existence. Your practical nature extends into every area of your life. As a student you can be diligent. As a business person you can be steady in pursuit of your goals. As a partner you can be pleasant, but can also hold your own in an argument. If you vacillate, it is in the area of financial security. You are always willing to earn more money. You take pleasure in the ordinary things of life.

Sun in Gemini

The essence of the air element is thinking. The essence of the mutable mode is flexibility. Thus Gemini exemplifies the adaptable mind. You thrive on change: change homes, change schools, change jobs, change your mind. You easily learn about everything you experience, thus you are a wonderful conversationalist. You want to experience and understand the entire world, but you may not be interested in the messy details.

As you cultivate a wide variety of interests, you begin to see that they are interrelated. Your capacity for thought eventually takes you deeper into certain subjects to explore them further. At the same time you recall information from a multitude of sources to support your thought process and decisions. You are a fine teacher because of this richness of information and your ability to recall it.

Sun in Cancer

The essence of the water element is feeling. The essence of the cardinal mode is action. Thus Cancer exemplifies active emotional participation in life. This does not mean that you are overemotional all the time. It does mean that you garner experiences on the feeling level—the gut level—early in life. This can develop into a stable emotional flow, as you understand the time and space relationships of people and things, and you can evaluate them internally, thus not revealing your judgment of situations until the proper time.

You want a positive, harmonious home. It can include a partner, children, or whatever, as long as you can relax and be comfortable. An intimate partner who understands you can be a great blessing. Lack of understanding can throw you into an emotional tailspin. The saying "Stay in the flow" was written for you, as you are like water flowing down the riverbed of life.

Sun in Leo

The essence of the fire element is intuition. The essence of the fixed mode is stability. Thus Leo exemplifies the substantive application of intuition in your life. You can become a strong leader through this one skill. The best leaders not only know what their goals are, they also understand how the people around them can help achieve the goals. Then they facilitate the best work of each individual. But first you have to learn how to manage yourself, and you do this through experiencing your intuition, taking action, and evaluating the results.

The creative energy of Leo can be likened to making pottery. Intuition suggests the future use of your product. Then you go about creating it. Finally, you temper it in the real or metaphorical fire that you find appropriate. Only then do you know that you have a good result. Progress in Leo's life is based on two things: personal ability and strong associations with others.

Sun in Virgo

The essence of the earth element is sensation. The essence of the mutable mode is flexibility. Thus Virgo exemplifies an adaptable approach to the material world. You have innate skills of manipulation. You can help yourself and others because you can see how to make meaningful changes without upsetting the entire system. Your methodical mind is willing to examine the details of a situation to find the gems of body, mind, and spirit within them. Then you work with other people, using the information you have gathered.

You learn early in life to identify things that are not working, and you have good ideas about how to fix them. You also learn that there is a compassionate way to communicate this information. Sometimes you only indicate an area of difficulty, and allow others to find their own mistakes. Because you strive for the correct behavior for each situation, you generally are capable of satisfactory communication with whomever you meet.

Sun in Libra

The essence of the air element is thinking. The essence of the cardinal mode is action. Thus Libra exemplifies active thought processes. Because Libra is about balance, this is a good time to point out that everyone has all four functions, and everyone can act in all three modes. Each Sun sign has a particular focus, and each chart has its own balance or imbalance of energies. For Libra to maximize the active thinking potential, considerations of all kinds of balance are brought under the umbrella of logical thought. You consider the social situation and exercise good manners. You adapt to the demands of the moment.

The desire for harmony and balance can lead to indecision. It's important to remember that balance is easier to achieve when you are in motion. Standing still actually demands a great deal of concentration and energy. Think of the high wire act. The acrobat is rarely still on the wire.

Your active mind provides you with the stuff of social skills, and therefore you develop strong associations with others throughout your life. This is easier when you direct your own course in a decisive manner. Relationships provide the fuel for your growth and development throughout life.

Sun in Scorpio

The essence of the water element is feeling. The essence of the fixed mode is stability. Thus Scorpio exemplifies profound depths of feeling. Internal bodily functions can provide a sensitive barometer of your effectiveness in the world. Fixed water can be ice—the unhappy Scorpio brings a chill to the emotional environment. Yet Scorpio can be the hottest ticket around, both sexually and emotionally. The way you control your passions dictates the way your life either freezes or flows. Hint: frozen is not nearly as much fun.

The depth of willpower is intense for the Scorpio Sun sign. You are fearless in situations other people walk—or run—away from. You may be wonderful in the moment of crisis, only to become emotional mush afterward. This happens because you draw on your emotional reserves too quickly and deeply, or because you overestimate your capabilities, or sometimes because you react instinctively and later snap back to reality. The important thing is that you can rise to the occasion when it is necessary, and you will be admired for this single trait.

Sun in Sagittarius

The essence of the fire element is intuition. The essence of the mutable mode is flexibility. Thus Sagittarius exemplifies the adaptability of the philosopher/teacher. You envision the future results of your actions, and you are able to plan carefully because you sense the outcomes quite clearly. People often come to you for advice because they value your foresight.

But you are not always so serious. You enjoy sports, and if not the sports themselves, the environment in which lively action occurs. You engage in a variety of outdoor and indoor physical activities. You may love being around horses.

One positive outcome of your flexible, intuitive style is that you form strong associations with other people, and you move steadily forward in life. Imagine the stillness of the winter solstice, when life has ebbed. You are there, considering the results of past actions and preparing for future developments. Even though Sagittarius is a fire sign, you generally make cool decisions.

Sun in Capricorn

The essence of the earth element is sensation. The essence of the cardinal mode is action. Thus Capricorn exemplifies active involvement in the physical world. You are a hard worker, keeping to the task until you achieve your goals. Career is more than a job for you—it is a vocation, and may be a spiritual mission as well. Because of the consistent effort you put into your work, you will achieve advancement. You are tough enough to withstand the struggle inherent in the business or professional world.

The Capricorn combination of action and practicality works because you understand yourself very well. Your sense of reality also extends to your own thoughts and feelings. You are cautious in your decisions, yet ambitious. This balance keeps you on the direct path you set for yourself. Your honesty and dependability may keep you from engaging in risky ventures, but these traits are the stuff of your reputation, and your reputation brings you promotions, or work if you are self-employed. While life isn't all about work, for you work can be the biggest slice of the pie.

Sun in Aquarius

The essence of the air element is thinking. The essence of the fixed mode is stability. Thus Aquarius exemplifies deep understanding that comes from consistent thought processes. You are a scientific thinker, even if your chief interests are not in the sciences. You take an unconventional approach to life and find new subjects and people interesting. You have the ability to gain cooperation from others, as long as you maintain some personal level of communication.

Not only are you a good observer, you have an intuitive sense of what is happening around you. You therefore plan for the future and see many of your plans coming true. You have a strong interest in metaphysical and occult subjects, and you never discard an idea just because it is strange—you work with it to see if it fits into your beliefs.

Sun in Pisces

The essence of the water element is feeling. The essence of the mutable mode is flexibility. Thus Pisces exemplifies the receptive and empathetic responses you have toward others. Your sensitivity can lead to the study of mystical teachings, and even into psychic realms. While you can slip into negativity in these areas, you are also capable of focusing on the cooperative, positive psychic input from the world around you. On the positive side, you can study mystical subjects and absorb knowledge easily.

You are somewhat retiring, preferring not to be in the forefront of many activities. You can seem secretive to others when you resist open participation. If you become reclusive, you miss out on the rich emotional possibilities that your receptive nature makes possible. You can turn your natural adaptability into an asset by accepting the fast pace of activities around you, at least part of the time.

The Fifth House—Home of the Sun

Traditional astrology has identified the Fifth House as the house of children, lovers, gamblers, and speculation. These people and activities all have creativity of one kind or another, and it is creativity that enlivens all the activities and people associated with this section of the chart.

Most activities can be understood as having a creative element. There are three distinct kinds of creativity: creation, recreation, and procreation.

Creation

All people are born with creative potential. Creativity is not limited to the arts—creative energy can be used in all forms of work, play, and relationships. The dictionary suggests that creativity is the process of making something—bringing something into existence. It involves something original, as compared to an imitation or copy. Creativity is also associated with imagination. To restrict our concept of creativity to the arts is to restrict our own joy. I personally feel creative when I help another person solve a problem, even when that problem has nothing to do with art.

Recreation

The word recreation literally means to create anew, to restore, to refresh. Recreation has come to mean activities, especially outdoor activities, that provide diversion; it also means hobbies. Spaces devoted to recreation are often oriented around social activities. So creativity here is about refreshing one's spirit through activities, either alone or in groups. Gambling can be viewed as a form of recreation, even for professionals, if it also has the associated characteristics of hobby, diversion, or social activity.

Procreation

There's no problem understanding this one. To procreate is to reproduce—it literally means to create forward (in time). We can become confused, though, when we confuse love with the simple procreative act of sex. While we all experience various kinds and levels of love, we can't define the profound feeling very well. It is clear that we can procreate without having or understanding love at all. Yet the act of loving another person is an ongoing expression of our highest and best creative potential.

The Creative Process

The Fifth House provides a picture of our creative potential in all three of these arenas. Any process that brings something new into existence is creative by definition. The planets and signs associated with this house will define the natural direction of your creativity.

The Fifth House is related to the heart and to the back (spine). We need the structure of the body/mind to shape new ideas and things, and we need the heart's desire to motivate us to create. A metaphorical heart and spine enhance our creative efforts.

We have considered the first of the planets, signs, and houses. Now let's take a look at the first and most significant of the aspects: the conjunction.

The Conjunction Aspect

To be conjunct is to be together in one place. The positions or points in a chart are measured in zodiacal longitude—the division of the zodiac into 360 degrees along the ecliptic (the apparent path of the Sun). Two planets are said to be conjunct when they are close to the same degree. What do we mean by close? Most astrologers say that planets are not conjunct unless they are within 6 degrees of each other. Many would use a smaller allowance (orb). Some would allow more, especially for the Sun and Moon.

When two planets are this close together, they highlight each other. Each of the planets has its own focused energy, but when they are together, first one is active—it is presented to the world by the other. Then the roles shift, and the second planet is more in the spotlight, being supported or stimulated by the first. Sometimes the two planets work so closely together that their energies are difficult to experience separately. This relationship reminds us of parent and child, lovers, or the creator and the idea. Each illuminates and enhances the other, and each is sustained by its partner as well.

Another facet of the conjunction relationship is that it represents the beginning and ending point of the circle of the zodiac. As such, a conjunction of planets suggests that the person will experience beginnings and endings in ways indicated by the particular planets. This is important. A conjunction of two warm, fuzzy planets will reflect different experiences than two harsh, hard-edged planets. Think about different kinds of relationships: If parent and child are compatible, even the beginning and endings they experience will be satisfactory. If lovers are together only for the sex and they are not compatible in other ways, the ending can be devastating. If the creator feels forced or out of harmony, the creation will reflect that feeling.

It is helpful to remember that every ending involves a new beginning. The ideal end of a pregnancy is a new life, and the ideal result of any creative effort is something that represents the feeling behind it fully and truthfully. When looking at a conjunction in a chart, then, you can identify a bit of each of the qualities: prominence, reflection, and endings and beginnings.

Many charts will not have a conjunction. When this happens, it does not mean you can't have a good experience of beginnings and endings. Instead, it means that beginnings and endings are not fundamentally slanted in a particular direction. Throughout your life you will experience them, but each time the experience will feel new.

Often beginnings and endings occur when a transiting planet conjoins a birth planet. *Transit* means where the planets actually are at a particular time. Your birthchart is a picture of the transits for the day and time you were born, for example. When a planet moves into the same degree as one in the birthchart, there is a sense of ending one cycle and beginning another. Thus even if a chart has no conjunctions, there will be new cycles coming into existence.

Case Study: Johannes Kepler

Johannes Kepler was a mathematical genius. He derived precise mathematical principles from observed data about the movement of the planets. He was also an astrologer of some note, and letters he wrote on the subject confirm that he read charts for people.

Kepler had three conjunctions in his birthchart: The Sun to Venus, Mercury to Uranus, and Jupiter to Pluto. Of course, when calculating his own chart, he would not have included Uranus, Neptune, or Pluto, as they had not yet been discovered when he was alive. He would only have seen the Sun-Mercury and Sun-Venus conjunctions. The Sun is in the Seventh House and Venus is in the Eighth House, but they are just over 3 degrees apart, and this is close enough to be a conjunction.

I have included two charts for Kepler (charts 6 and 7) to show the most popular styles of charts. The first shows the houses to be the same size (equal house), while the second shows the houses unequal in size. The chart wheels in the CD-ROM program and the charts in this book are all equal house.

What can we say about Kepler as an individual? Can we identify his chart as being that of a mathematical genius? Let's look at what we have learned so far.

Sun in Capricorn

In this chapter we found that the Sun in Capricorn indicates an individual whose mode is action in the material realm (cardinal earth). Kepler was such a person, diligently pursuing his interest in mathematics. He was a student of Pythagoras, and he wanted to confirm the theories of his teacher as applied to the solar system. He held a variety of positions during his life and climbed to the positions of Court Mathematician and Court Astrologer from his childhood peasant beginnings.

Sun in the Seventh House

Kepler did not work alone. He had a patron throughout most of his career, and was employed as the Court Mathematician for Emperor Rudolf II, King of Bohemia, and later as Court Astrologer for Albrecht Wallenstein, a Bohemian general. Before he held these positions, he was employed by Tycho Brahe and was a professor of mathematics.

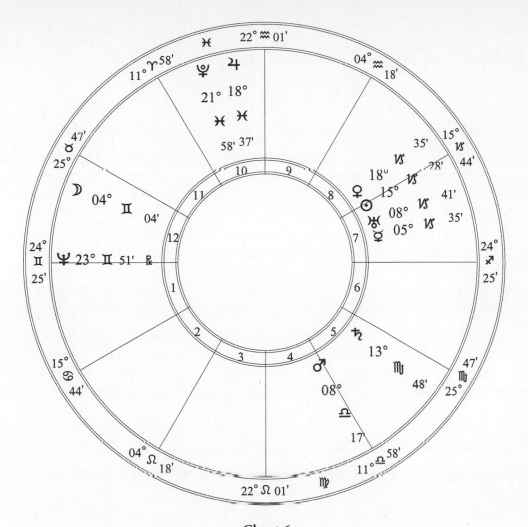

Chart 6
Johannes Kepler, Equal Houses
December 27, 1571 / Weil der Stadt, Germany / 2:37 P.M. LMT
Koch Houses

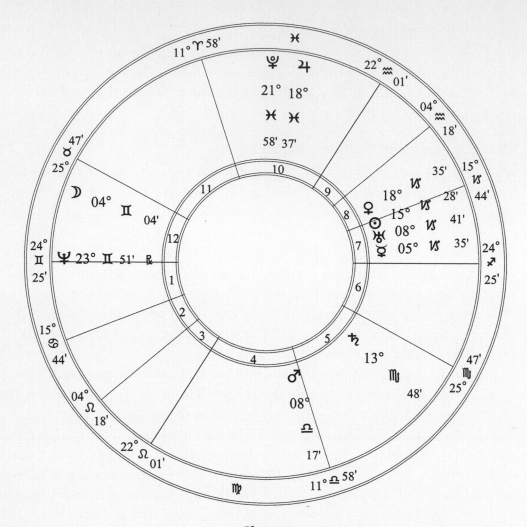

Chart 7
Johannes Kepler, Unequal Houses
December 27, 1571 / Weil der Stadt, Germany / 2:37 P.M. LMT
Koch Houses

Libra on the Fifth-House Cusp

In the previous chapter on the zodiac, we learned that the sign Libra is all about balance. Kepler's creativity leans in that direction, as he sought balance through logical thought, another Libra characteristic. His creativity also depended on the background of Libra cooperation and partnership.

Saturn in Scorpio in the Fifth House

Saturn is the planet associated with Capricorn, Kepler's Sun sign. In the Fifth House, Saturn indicates creative attention to structure. Kepler's life work was to study the structure of the universe and, more particularly, the solar system.

Sun Conjunct Venus

Venus, the planet associated with Libra, and therefore with the Fifth House in Kepler's chart, is conjunct the Sun. Kepler's individuality is prominently connected to his sense of social conditions and with his value system. Thus we can conclude that Kepler pursued his individual aims through social channels, and that his values were closely associated with his individual interest in mathematics.

You can follow Kepler's chart, or any chart, through this book, building a body of information about the individual. Something to keep in mind as you go along is that while you are a twenty-first-century person, Kepler lived in the sixteenth and early seventeenth centuries—300 years ago. Not only did he not know about the outer planets in our solar system, he and his contemporaries were not certain of basic orbital mechanics. They didn't have computers, televisions, airplanes, or any of our modern conveniences. Travel was slow. People died young of all sorts of diseases. Even though the chart factors are the same, try to think of Kepler in the cultural, economic, and social life of Europe 400 years ago. This will help you understand his chart and how it relates to him. The same is true for charts you do for yourself and friends. Remember the familial, cultural, and economic realities of the person whose chart you are considering.

Exercise

Now that you have a few building blocks for the chart, take some time to look at your own chart. If you haven't already done so, use your CD-ROM program now to create your birthchart.

1. Find the Sun. What sign is it in? What is the element and mode? Re-read the myth associated with this sign. What does that tell you about yourself that you may not have thought about before?

2. Look at the Fifth House. What signs are there? Remember, there is a sign on the cusp (edge) of each house, and sometimes there is a whole sign inside the house. (For example, if you look back at George W. Bush's chart, you will see that he has entire signs inside his Fourth and Tenth Houses.) Each of these signs says something about your activities in the area of your life indicated by the Fifth House—creativity in all its forms.

3. Are there any planets in the Fifth House? If so, consider keywords for them.

4. Are there any planets close enough together to say they are conjunct? What does it mean for you to have a conjunction? What if you don't have one?

Summary

By now you are already thinking about the Sun in your chart. If it isn't in the Fifth house, what house is it in? If there are other planets in the Fifth House, you may also be curious about what they mean. This book describes the planets, houses, and aspects in a particular order. You can skip ahead by looking at the table of contents to explore additional planets, houses, and aspects.

We have considered the Sun, the Fifth House, and the conjunction aspect. Next we turn to the Moon, the Fourth House, and how the Sun and Moon work together in the chart.

4
The Moon and the Fourth House

Where the Sun reflects your individuality, the Moon reflects the less conscious part of your personality. Its position in the birthchart can tell a lot about where your emotional stress comes from, and how you react instead of consciously responding to events and situations. The Moon is also where you find information about how you assimilate and store information—about how you learn and about how your memory functions.

The Moon represents the feminine in a chart (along with Venus). The maternal instinct, in both men and women, is seen through the Moon's position, along with emotional traits in general. While many of the Moon's traits have been delegated to women in the past, in our twenty-first-century culture we are more accepting of exchanging roles. It remains true that procreation depends on male and female sexual roles, but very few other activities require one or the other of the sexes. By the same token, men can be just as receptive and nurturing as women. Modern psychology has taught us not to limit ourselves to prescribed masculine and feminine roles.

In any astrological chart the Moon represents the action. In a person's chart the Moon indicates how that individual instinctually acts, and it further indicates how events will unfold. In charts for events, the Moon reveals the action, based on the nature of the event. Because the Moon is the fastest-moving point in the chart, it can be used as a timing device for our daily, monthly, and longer cycles.

The Moon indicates the means we use in our daily activities. We have one type of individuality, indicated by the Sun, and often a quite different method for accomplishing our goals. Later in this chapter, after looking at the Moon in the signs and at the Fourth House, we will consider the Sun and Moon together as a team. By looking at just these two points in the chart, you can learn a lot about how you fulfill your desires and needs.

The Moon Through the Signs

Now we will look at how we assimilate information, nurture others, and respond to instincts.

Moon in Aries

The Moon, being less conscious, is likely to take action rather impulsively. Always changeable—think of the monthly lunar cycle and the changing face of the Moon—in Aries it becomes even hastier. There may be arguments and sudden shifts of opinion.

The Moon in Aries also reflects a personality bent on personal control. Such a person acts in a willful way, often without regard for anyone else. In fact, action is taken without much regard for the self either. This can come across as a carefree approach to life, but it can also be reckless. On the positive side, the receptive nature of the Moon makes intuition flow easily. If you listen to intuition before hastily taking action, then you receive the benefit of understanding the invisible energies around you, and you have a better eye for the future as well.

Moon in Taurus

Taurus is fixed earth. The Moon is said to be quite comfortable in this sign, which makes sense. The earth needs water to nourish plants, and the Moon is a watery sort of planet. The Moon's receptivity finds a sympathetic place in earth. The flowing nature of the Moon finds a stable container—the changeable Moon finds stability in this fixed sign.

The downside is that the watery nature either sinks into the ground of Taurus to nurture, or it runs off and forms first a stream, then a river. This water metaphor, when applied to the emotional nature, suggests that emotions can carry us away, or that they escape our mental container at times. When the Moon's nature escapes control, it can overindulge in food, spend too much money, or otherwise dissipate one's material possessions.

The more positive expression focuses on the nurturing capacity of this placement. There is constancy of activity needed to cultivate plants, helping them grow. The Taurus Moon also cultivates ideas, allowing them to take root in a protected environment. There is appreciation for the material world that allows us to collect beautiful things and care for them. And amid all this, there is a capacity to enjoy life fully and to share that enjoyment with others.

Moon in Gemini

The Moon's changeability is amplified in this mutable air sign. With the thinking function somewhat less conscious, there is an almost instinctive desire to communicate with the world. This can lead to a rather wishful existence that lacks stability and practicality. By the same token, wishes precede action. Desire can result in nurturing mental activity.

The Moon in Gemini reflects the capacity to express feelings in many ways. A change of mood provides a new set of parameters for writing or conversation, thus you are an interesting companion and guest. With your many interests, you may appear superficial at times—who has the time to delve deeply into so many subjects? However, your broad interests weave themselves together into an eclectic package, providing you with skills that can be applied to a variety of careers, social situations, and personal pursuits.

This placement of the Moon is an indicator of changes. Your life will be filled with different jobs, residences, and even unique travels. Therefore it is important to cultivate a nurturing quality within yourself—something that is portable and comfortable.

Moon in Cancer

Traditionally the Moon is associated with the sign of Cancer.[1] The element is water and the mode is cardinal, or active. On the physical plane this is the very essence of water flowing downhill. It moves at the rate that the slope and gravity allow. Because there is a natural flow, the person with Moon in Cancer is emotionally strong and consistent. Whenever this emotional current is disrupted, there can be digestive problems. Thus the body acts as a barometer for the emotional weather and signals when it is time to relax, rest, and regain objectivity.

Domestic relationships of all kinds are important with Moon in Cancer. Whether you live with parents, children, spouse, or friends, the home environment is a primary influence on your state of mind. Less is more in the home department. You can have comfortable, beautiful things around you, but it is more important to have organization and neatness. You can be happy just by meeting your own basic needs. Because you have a good sense of "flow" in all areas of your life, you are good at making sure that home is a safe, comfortable spot.

Moon in Leo

Here we have a fixed fire sign trying to accommodate a watery planet. In general this is not a comfortable combination, but neither is it a very uncomfortable one. The Moon is amenable to the intuitive influences indicated by Leo, making for a confident emotional state. Unlike the simple tastes of the Moon in Cancer, Moon in Leo likes luxury and surrounds itself with the finer things of life. If this tendency goes too far, the individual becomes snobbish, believing others are beneath him or her.

The passionate nature seeks expression and support. Some of the vanity just mentioned might actually be insulation against what other people say or do. Because the Moon in Leo indicates responsible positions gained through merit, one can figure that responsibility extends to sensitive treatment of others. While it is hard for people with this placement to admit they are wrong, when they do it is sincere and heartfelt, and accompanied by an effort to do better.

Moon in Virgo

This mutable earth sign welcomes the watery energy of the Moon. Earth and water are always a good combination when both are functioning in a positive way. The Virgo Moon reflects the capacity for the mind to take the driver's seat. You make practical considerations in your work and in relationships, leaving emotional considerations for others. You feel best when you are diligent in your work and when you follow Miss Manner's rule book.

You can become boring. This is because you are actually very predictable when you stick to the "rules." Other planets in your chart are where you find the spice in life, and Moon in Virgo is where you organize those spices so you can choose which ones to use in today's dishes. Underneath your practicality there lives a somewhat sensitive digestive system, so order and care are important to your emotional well-being.

Moon in Libra

Your soul seeks harmony and balance in everything you do. You are very capable of expressing your feelings and desires, and you seek close companionship or partnership to help provide balance. Once you have the closeness, you tend to become dependent on it, expecting the other person to make decisions so that you don't have to. Then you are freed up to be sociable and outgoing.

Sometimes people see you as irresponsible, due to the fact that you let other people do so much for you. It is very important for you to choose your associates carefully. The best relationships involve people who are supportive, but who don't let you lean on them too much. Codependence is not good for any relationship. Interdependence, where sharing is balanced, is far better.

Moon in Scorpio

Scorpio is the fixed water sign, and the Moon is a watery planet. Together they make for deep channels in midstream, where emotions can create an undertow, drawing you into more and more intense situations. One expression of emotion is the tendency to come out fighting. Small situations can seem as critical as a near-drowning out in deep water with no one close enough to help.

When this emotional depth has been explored, you will find that you are nothing if not truthful. Yes, you are sometimes tactless. But you feel that total honesty is better than little lies and bent truths that mislead and perhaps even cause great harm. In that same current you find the energy and desire to survive whatever the world throws at you. When others are out for the count, you surface again with renewed strength.

Moon in Sagittarius

You are changeable in a whole different way from the Moon in Scorpio. First of all you are moody, even fickle in your desires. Part of you relies on a consistent beacon of spiritual light that guides your decisions. Another part of you goes whenever and wherever you want, with a casual disregard for others. These two paths need to come together and form a clear road into the future. Otherwise you scatter your energies and never accomplish much of anything.

When you are on track in a positive direction, your natural optimism overflows, cheering up everyone around you. You are able to inspire others to do their best work.

Partly this is because you show that you care deeply about their success. Partly it is because you take the same attitude toward your own work most of the time. You experience a lot of changes, yet your primary direction remains clear.

Moon in Capricorn

The Moon is not so comfortable in Capricorn. The Moon wants things to flow easily and consistently, while Capricorn, the cardinal earth sign, wants to construct physical monuments and concrete evidence of what is true and right. You are happiest when you have a goal and you work to achieve it. Instead of always being responsible for others, let them support you once in a while.

The best thing for you to do is to find a profession you truly enjoy. It can be ambitious in scope as long as it really satisfies your inner emotional needs. Of course, you have to look at your emotional needs in order to know if they are being satisfied. You can do this self-examination in private and maintain your practical exterior. Just be sure to take the time to listen to your own needs on a regular basis (once a day or week, not once a year).

Moon in Aquarius

The Moon is effective here, as the feeling nature is associated closely with the mental nature. You have all sorts of ideas about what you want and how to get it. You are, from the beginning, what the police would call a trained observer. You tend to notice everything, including the emotional tone of situations, turns of phrase, dress, and demeanor. You are therefore able to draw the shy one into a conversation or take time to listen to special requests.

At the same time you have your own desires, and you want someone to listen to them. You are more capable of change than many people. You expect others to adapt to your needs and may be surprised when they balk. After all, to you fair is fair. Experience teaches you to offer help freely, with no strings attached. You take pleasure in your offer, not in what you get in return.

Moon in Pisces

This is a very fluid combination that can lead to problems if it is not balanced by other influences in the chart. If you are wide open to the psychic and emotional energies of other people, you feel drained of your own essence. Instead of adapting to whatever other people want, you need to devise a way to hold your own ground. If you have this placement, you may be saying, "Yeah, right. How do I do that?"

One way is to look to the Sun in your chart. The Sun is good at taking a leadership role. It likes to be in charge. If you can get your Sun and Moon to share, with the Pisces Moon providing information about feelings and the Sun, wherever it is, providing a container for those feelings, you are good to go. Even with the Sun in Pisces, you can align your feelings and your authority. If you are just a bit bolder in expressing your own feelings, you create an atmosphere where exchange is mutually supportive.

The Fourth House—Home of the Moon

The Fourth House is the foundation of the chart. Resting at a point opposite the Midheaven, it is the place where all your thoughts and feelings eventually gather. In the end, you will evaluate your entire life on the basis of the beliefs you cultivate throughout the years. As the foundation point, the Fourth House indicates home, family, and core beliefs.

Home

Let's consider the home first. Except for a few very unfortunate individuals, we all have a home. It may be a one-room domicile, or it may be a mansion. This is the place we identify as home. It may not actually be where we live. During college we may still think of our parents' house as home. While traveling on assignment, we have a place to stay, but home is elsewhere. We may even live in a particular area for years, but when we speak of home, it is where we grew up or where some of our family members live.

All that said, home is the place where you feel comfortable with your ideas and feelings. It is the place where you can do whatever you want and not worry about what other people may think. It is the actual physical location where you are best able to nurture yourself and your immediate family, and it is a place where your beliefs "fit."

Family

Many of us had an early family life that was less than satisfactory. Others fondly recall their childhood and teen years and feel that home could not have been much better. The deepest feelings about home tend to center around those people who formed the nuclear family group. This group is somewhat flexible in its composition. For example, I had a mother, father, and two siblings—the standard sort of family. Two changes in that group come to mind. When I was young, I went to stay at my aunt's house for about two weeks. I remember that I was treated just like the rest of the kids. I was part of my aunt's family for that two weeks. My grandmother lived with my family for many years. While she was there, she was definitely part of the nuclear family. When she lived somewhere else she was just Grandma. Our perceptions of family are quite flexible.

Core Beliefs

There are two kinds of core beliefs. First there are beliefs we learn as children from our family, from the social environment, and perhaps from religious practices. Generally we are instructed in basic beliefs, and we later find it is nearly impossible to sort them out from what we actually think is true. We may bump up against such a belief and wonder why it seems so strange, yet we act upon it almost from instinct. For example, suppose that your parents taught you that cleanliness is next to godliness. Imagine a grandparent coming to live with you who is not so rigidly dedicated to the daily details of house cleaning. How do you reconcile the difference in belief? You have the basic habit of putting away your toys as soon as you are finished playing with them, and Grandpa says, "Oh, leave it for later. It will still be there when we get home." An attractive idea, yet you put the toy away.

Let's take a more serious example. Suppose your parents come from different religious backgrounds. You may be required to attend a particular church, but you soon learn that some of your relatives believe something different. You have bumped up against the core beliefs you have been taught. This sets the stage for you to think through your own ideas and ideals.

The second set of core beliefs are those we develop through study and consideration, or insights that come upon us suddenly at critical junctures in our lives. Major events, traumatic or otherwise, often cause us to rethink what we have been taught and to explore what lies at the heart of our own true beliefs. To use the cleanliness example, I do still find that if I put things away properly, I later know where to find them. And I deeply dislike unnecessary clutter. However, I don't feel the need to instantly wipe up every little speck of dirt that is tracked into the house. Instead I like a regular routine for mopping and vacuuming. In addition, I have turned loose the concept that I am responsible for all the details. At the same time, I find it nearly impossible to allow a small child to "mess up" every room of my house. I want some order somewhere. You could say that the childhood precept of neatness stuck to me.

To take our more serious example, once we begin to question the core beliefs we have been taught, we either find them to be suitable or not. If they don't suit us, we may go on our own odyssey of exploration into a wide range of religious and philosophical studies. In search of deeper meaning that suits us as individuals, we often find that some of what we were taught continues to make sense, while other tenets need to change.

The Fourth House, its sign, and planets in this house all indicate the ways in which home, family, and core beliefs operate in our lives. The three are woven tightly together for most of us. Home is where we find family, and family is the source of our first information about the world. Beliefs are rooted in this context. We can trim the vines of belief, but we need to nurture the roots. Seldom do we tear up the plant so completely that tiny sprouts will not appear later.

The Sun and Moon As a Team

Science teaches us that the Sun is a huge, very hot object, and that the Moon is a much smaller, cold one. However, what we experience is that the Moon and Sun are the same size. This means that when the Moon passes directly between the Sun and Earth, we experience a solar eclipse. When the Earth passes between the Sun and Moon, we experience a lunar eclipse. These eclipses occur with striking regularity, in nineteen-year patterns or cycles. The astrological significance of this pattern is revealed in the joint functions of the Sun and Moon.

Conscious and Unconscious

The Sun represents consciousness, and the Moon represents the less conscious side of our minds. When the Sun is eclipsed, we experience a moment of profound unconsciousness. For the eclipse to have this personal effect, it must occur in the same degree as a planet in our own chart. Then we feel the shift in awareness relative to the energy of the planet involved. Similar to the phases of the Moon, we experience a longer cycle of phases. When the Sun has moved one-fourth, one-half, and three-quarters of the way through the zodiac (when the Sun forms the square and opposition aspects to the place where the eclipse occurred), then we may experience mental fuzziness or a lack of conscious awareness.

Something similar happens with lunar eclipses. This time there is a momentary disconnection from unconscious processes. The cycle is played out over the next month in the same way the Sun takes a full year to complete one phase cycle. To a certain extent each lunar phase connects us to the less conscious natural processes of life.

Animus and Anima

The Sun and Moon represent the animus and anima within each of us. The Sun is the more conscious factor, and the Moon is the less conscious factor. For men the Sun is the animus, and for women it may represent the anima, or feminine function of the psyche. For the Moon it is the opposite. The conscious side generally functions well, but the unconscious component can present some problems.

Spirit and Form

The Sun reflects Spirit, while the Moon is the essence of form, connected as it is to digestion and assimilation processes. Because the Sun provides us with a picture of what spirit means for each individual, it should be no surprise that as we grow and learn, we continue to return to the sign in which our birth Sun resides. We find our true strength there. We spend a lifetime exploring all the other energies available to us. In the end, we seek to express the best and highest qualities of our Sun sign. Modern astrology begins with Sun sign information.

Case Study: Celine Dion

Celine Dion has both the Sun and Moon in Aries. When the Sun and Moon are in the same sign, there is a close alignment of the individuality and vitality, reflected by the Sun, with the subconscious emotionality and inner personal strength, reflected by the Moon.

We saw in the previous chapter that the Sun in Aries reflects assertiveness that can even be aggressive. There is strong intuition that informs decisions and actions. The individual is directed, perhaps even one-pointed. These qualities affect the creative process, as the Sun is associated with the Fifth House of creativity.

Celine's Sun is conjunct the Midheaven and Saturn. Although we have not yet discussed these two points in depth, chapter 1 gave us the keywords of *self-awareness* for the Midheaven and *structure* for Saturn. Celine thus is self-aware and makes practical

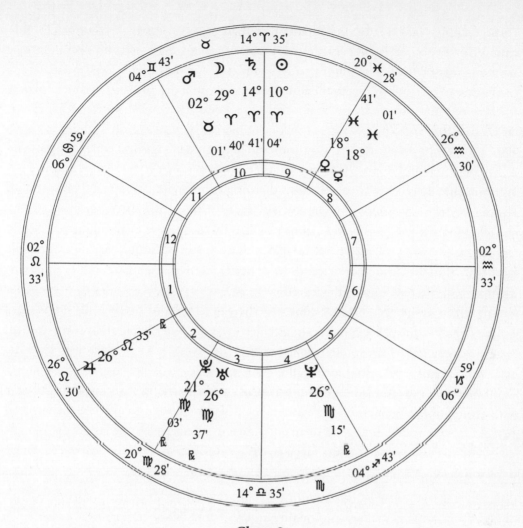

Chart 8
Celine Dion
March 30, 1968 / Charlemagne, Québec / 12:15 P.M. EST
Koch Houses

considerations right along with her Aries directedness and assertiveness. For her, the distinction between self-awareness and structure may not be important—she may see them as one and the same thing.

We haven't examined the Ninth House yet either. With the Sun here, Celine probably focuses on philosophy, religion, and travel a great deal. We were all aware of her extensive travels, but most people were surprised at her decision to leave her career to spend time with her husband after he was diagnosed with cancer. This decision was grounded in her personal philosophy concerning family and marriage. The outcome of the decision was that her creativity turned toward having children and enjoying them with her husband—two expressions of creativity that are very different from her singing career.

The Moon is also in Aries in Celine's chart. In this chapter we learned that the Moon indicates somewhat less conscious mental activity. It can be impulsive. A lot of people probably thought Celine's decision to leave her career was impulsive and even downright stupid. After all, who quits when they are at the very top? Another side of the Aries Moon is the desire for personal control. When her husband became ill, she was no longer able to control every aspect of her destiny. One way to maintain some control was to choose to spend as much time with him as possible. This decision reflects the selfless nature of Aries impulsiveness too.

While the Aries Sun is in the Ninth House, the Aries Moon is in the Tenth House. For Celine, career is an emotional outlet. She puts her heart into every recording and performance. Social standing is also an emotional draw, and marriage is part of one's social standing. Celine takes her marriage just as seriously as she takes her career, evidently even more so.

Case Study: Tiger Woods

Tiger Woods has the Sun in Capricorn and the Moon in Sagittarius. In chapter 3 we learned that the Sun in Capricorn reflects the sensation function, or connection to the material world. The cardinal expression relates to action. Tiger exemplifies mastery of the physical world in his golf game. He works hard to maintain the best-quality game possible, and we see his individuality in both the smile he offers frequently and the looks of concern and even irritation when his shots don't go the way he planned.

In this chapter we read about the Fourth House, where Tiger's Sun is found. Home and family are powerful considerations for him. His parents are strong influences and have guided his career, as well as his personal growth and development. We don't know

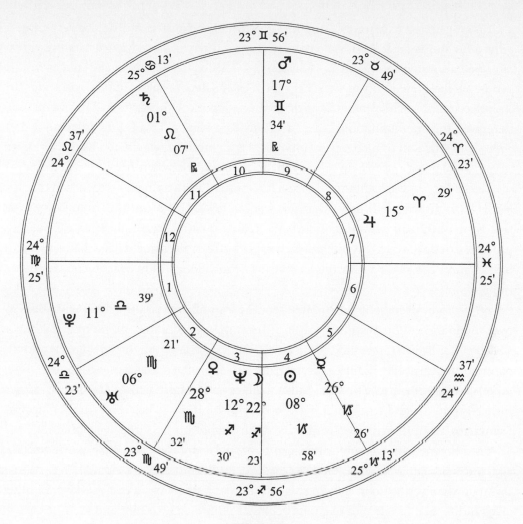

Chart 9
Tiger Woods
December 30, 1975 / Long Beach, CA / 10:50 P.M. PST
Koch Houses

a lot about his core beliefs because he keeps them to himself. We do, however, know quite a bit about Tiger Woods the person. Not yet thirty years old, Tiger has already established a foundation called *Start Something*. This organization reaches out to young people aged eleven to fourteen to "help them establish core values, create goals, identify strategies for the achievement of their goals, and work with mentors."[2] In the mission statement for the foundation, Tiger mentions core values. This is how important they are to him. His Sun in the Fourth House uses the ambition reflected in Capricorn both for personal goals and to help others achieve their highest potential.

Tiger's Moon is in Sagittarius in the Third House. In this chapter we learned that the Moon in Sagittarius indicates a changeable, even fickle attitude. It is hard to know what you want. At the same time there is a fairly steady spiritual beacon that guides you. This paradox can be hard to live with unless you get both on the same track. Change is a part of life, and even more so for the Sagittarius Moon, so a steady beacon can be a good thing.

While Tiger presents a positive role model for us all, he was once a kid with ideas all over the map, and his map had golf in it from the age of about six months. He was a skilled golfer by age three, and there is no doubt that he has both the intelligence and the natural physical ability required for the game. I recall what a friend once told me: "Tiger Woods is a genuinely nice person." Some qualities he was born with, and some he learned from his parents and teachers. Tiger is a Buddhist and practices meditation, reflecting Sagittarius in a different way (see also the discussion of his Neptune in chapter 12).

The Sun and Moon combine for Tiger to produce ambition and drive, along with the ability to withstand his rigorous travel, practice, and tournament schedule. Tiger thinks through whatever he does, allowing his intuition to guide him, in golf as well as in other areas of life. His family and religious beliefs are important to him and are reflected in the way he lives his life.

Exercise

You can see that just a little bit of information about astrology can take you a long way toward understanding yourself and the people around you. As we move through the book, we will add more planets, houses, and aspects to our understanding of these two charts.

1. Find the Moon and the Fourth House in your chart. What do they indicate?

2. Compare what you learned about the Sun and Fifth House with what you know about the Moon and Fourth House. How do they blend together? How do they indicate different sides of the personality?

3. What questions does the comparison raise in your mind? You may want to list the questions and check them off as they are answered in the following chapters.

Summary

The Sun and Moon are the most prominent objects in the day and night sky. Metaphorically they are the most significant objects in your horoscope. Together they describe the basics of your physical being, emotional life, mental style, and spiritual potential. As we look at the other planets and the aspects they make, we develop a well-rounded set of tools for understanding ourselves as whole beings. Along the way you will find more exercises designed to provide a holistic approach to astrology.

---

1. See the table in chapter 1 that shows the signs associated with each of the planets (or refer to the chart you made in the exercise in chapter 1).

2. For more information, see http://www.twfound.org.

5
The Ascendant
and Your Persona

What Is the Persona?

A lot has been written about the Ascendant, considering it on every level from physical appearance to spiritual expression. I have chosen a few quotations from contemporary and historical works on the subject to make some specific points.

Noel Tyl, in his book *Synthesis and Counseling in Astrology*, states that "the Ascendant is always like an echo or expansion or modification of the Sun-Moon blend."[1] This has at least two meanings. First, the Ascendant is part of a chart that contains a particular Sun and Moon, and it does not function independently of them. For example, if you have the Sun in Taurus and Ascendant in Aquarius, then you have a largely Taurean individuality from which your Aquarian persona operates.

Secondly, the sign on the Ascendant indicates a focus for your life, beyond the Sun and Moon signs. The Aquarian Ascendant indicates how you express yourself in the world, and because how you act has an effect on you, it colors the way you see the world. In *Astrology: Understanding the Birth Chart*, Kevin Burk states, "The Ascendant has been described as 'the mask we wear' when we relate to other people. The thing about this mask, though, is that it also colors the way we see the world."[2]

So how do we develop our Ascendant-based persona? In *Choice Centered Astrology*, Gail Fairfield says, "The sign on the Ascendant represents the qualities that were most reinforced by your whole extended family system."[3] Take our Aquarian Ascendant as an example. On the one side are characteristics of restlessness, rebellion, eccentric behavior, and a lack of sympathy for other individuals. As a child, your parents and teachers would very likely have steered you away from these qualities and toward other Aquarian qualities like altruism, friendliness, persistence in mental tasks, and cooperation. While you might not completely give up your capacity to rebel, you very likely took the somewhat easier path of fitting in. Since persona is about expressing yourself, you have these kinds of choices.

In *New Mansions for New Men*, Dane Rudhyar associated the breath with the First House. This is completely logical, in that the Ascendant is a point on the eastern horizon at the time the infant draws its first breath. The Ascendant and Midheaven are both points that are determined solely by the place and time of birth, and they are therefore very personal points in the chart. (The Midheaven is discussed in chapter 15.)

On the more spiritual plane, Alice Bailey, in *Esoteric Astrology*, says that the Ascendant, or the rising sign, "indicates the remoter possibilities, and the spiritual goal and purpose of the immediate incarnation."[4] We are not focusing on spirituality as it relates to astrology; however, it is important to note that the Ascendant does reflect the immediate purpose for one's lifetime. While we all are seeking the best expression of the Sun sign, we very often come to that higher expression through our rising sign and its influence.

The Ascendant Is Not the Sun or the Moon

The Ascendant is not the same as the Sun or Moon, or any other planet, for that matter. In chapter 3, we found that the Sun indicates your individuality—who and what you actually are, rough and unvarnished. You have your good and bad points, strengths and weaknesses, indicated by the Sun sign. In chapter 4, we learned that there is an undercurrent of less conscious activity that is represented by the Moon. The Moon also indicates how your nature, as shown by the Sun, will express in your life. The Moon suggests what is likely to happen and how you are likely to make personal decisions.

The Ascendant indicates how you show yourself to others and what you choose to show. Remember the mask. You are on stage throughout your whole life, and the Ascendant indicates the sort of character you generally play. To the extent that you play this role well or badly, the Ascendant also indicates how you tend to see the world. A well-played role will obtain happy results, and you are likely to feel the world is an accommodating place. Poorly or maliciously acted, you will find the world far less accommodating to your needs and desires.

The Ascendant Through the Signs

Ascendant in Aries

First and foremost, the personality expresses Aries energy through the will to assert the self in the environment. You are perceived to be materially ambitious. At the same time you have the capacity to assert yourself on the intuitive plane. This means that you are able to think well ahead in whatever activity you choose, as well as to apply your energy in the present moment. Thus people see you as a good planner.

People also see that you are courageous. You are able to engage in difficult situations, and you even let a bit of your fiery spirit out—you demonstrate your leadership potential by taking on big problems to solve. It is your lively, energetic personality that attracts people to you, and it is your intuitive vision that convinces them to trust you.

On the negative side, you have a quick temper. It is difficult for you to hide this fact. Along with it you sometimes come across as egotistical in your leadership style. These two qualities do not endear you to others. To compensate for these, you can cultivate a very different side of Aries energy—compassion. This may not be the easiest thing for you to do, as it is not the first impulse that springs into your mind. However, your intuition shows you future possibilities, among them how other people are likely to respond in a given situation. You consider likely outcomes and modify your present attitude and approach to achieve better future relationships.

A healthy effect of your more compassionate attitude is that you don't burn up your energy in irritation and anger. Instead you moderate the flow of energy so that your actions become more effective. You will find that you don't tire as easily. You may have fewer headaches. You find that meditation, even for a few minutes each day, releases tension that serves no practical purpose. Yet you can wind up to peaks of tension when that is desirable.

Ascendant in Taurus

The Taurus Ascendant generally expresses the personality more harmoniously than Aries. The forceful, ambitious drive is replaced by a steady, stick-to-it energy. People see you as reliable and thorough in all of your activities. You can be depended on to consider all the angles as you pursue your work.

You have strong desires, and this shows in your personality. When you present an idea, people see the practical potential, and they see the intent to bring the idea to fruition. Your typical expression of desires brings very different results: If you selfishly demand everything you want, people will find you difficult to live with. If, on the other hand, you demand only what you must have, request what you want, and demonstrate that you understand and appreciate the needs of others, you will manage quite nicely.

On a practical basis, you thrive when you own your own home, when your home is comfortable and secure, and when you pay attention to the details that assure its stability. You don't really need indulgent luxuries, although you enjoy a little something extra from time to time. Just as you take care of your home, you also take care of your physical body. When you are healthy, you are happy, regardless of your material circumstances.

Ascendant in Gemini

The Gemini Ascendant usually has two rather different faces to the personality. People see the cheerful, flexible, versatile side of your personality on a regular basis. This side has the advantages of fitting into a group and enriching social interchange. Another side of the persona is the intellectual. You are capable of exploring multiple subjects and multiple careers. You thrive when you have several things going on at all times. Yours is not a one-track mind.

You also thrive on mobility. You travel well, unlike Taurus, who may enjoy the destination, but not the trip. Mental travels include reading, email or other correspondence, and flights of fancy of all kinds. Others may believe you are always diplomatic, never sad, and generally agreeable. A few people get to see you when you are self-absorbed, grumpy, and too superficial to get a grip on life. Yet they find both sides of your personality lovable, and they know you will change your tune soon enough.

Your expression in the world is strongest when you have integrated several beliefs, skills, and intentions into one package. In this way you become more of a one-track person, while bringing many threads into your single weave. Some body/mind training can be very helpful, as you benefit from learning how to focus on one activity at a time. A martial art like Aikido provides grounding, develops strength of mind and body, and opens you to the spiritual side of your nature.

Ascendant in Cancer

The Cancer Ascendant indicates a personal focus on the home and the family. You actively work to make your home the proverbial castle—the décor and use of space reflect your personal emotions. You enjoy spending time at home with family and want everything arranged to suit the activities of each family member.

Cancer rising is sensitive to the feeling tones of others. You often see into important issues without being told the details. You employ a sympathetic style in consulting with others. The key to your own development has been the consistent effort to identify feelings you are getting from others as different from feelings that come from within yourself. Once you do this, you are able to work with others without being overwhelmed.

You have a sound work ethic. You go out into the world with the idea that you will work hard and make progress in a concrete way. Like water flowing downhill, you allow your energy to flow into the container of your work, your play, and your family. When the energy is flowing, you are contented and dedicated. If the flow stops, you become moody, and you seek a way to get things moving again. You discover that "acting out" is not the best method.

Ascendant in Leo

You are impressive. In fact, people see you as somewhat bigger than life. You may not aspire to be that big, but they see your value anyway. Some astrologers suggest that the Leo Ascendant is egocentric, even arrogant. That is one possible expression of this Ascendant, but it is not all there is, or even the most likely expression. You do enjoy splendid surroundings, no doubt about that. You also welcome others into your splendid palace and treat them like honored guests.

Remember, Leo is the fire element expressing in the fixed mode. We have discussed how this combination doesn't make sense on the surface. However, it does when we look at the basics. Leo is inspired and intuitive. You see into the future, into the spiritual realm, and into other people. How others see you is totally dependent on how you communicate what you gain through intuition. Self-confidence is a given. An open-minded attitude goes a long way to overcome the perception of self-absorption.

You are generous and fair. You personally thrive in an atmosphere where people are rewarded appropriately, whether at work, at home, or in social situations. Therefore you develop a style of rewarding others, even if the reward is simple praise for their efforts.

Ascendant in Virgo

Virgo on the Ascendant reflects your desire for stable surroundings. You need a stable situation so that your flexibility doesn't carry you away from key tasks and attitudes. When you have this stability, you thrive personally, and you are able to support family, friends, and coworkers as well. As you thrive, you are able to give due attention to all the important areas of your life.

Others feel they can come to you for help and advice. They see you as very capable of gathering the detailed information you need and then thinking through to a solution. They may not have the patience to consider the details the way you do, so they value your ability in this regard.

You can take a critical attitude when needed. Sometimes this comes across as petty or fussy and may not be appreciated in the spirit you intended. You can provide a far more detailed analysis of each tiny misstep than people want to hear. You become a better parent, friend, and manager when you master the fine art of the one-minute reprimand. Most people get as much as they care to hear in one minute, and you get the problem out in the open.

Ascendant in Libra

You thrive when your base of operations is harmonious and even elegant. Your home or office doesn't require the most expensive furnishings, but you do need everything to fit together nicely. Then you become the social director of the best meetings and get-togethers. Your good manners and thoughtful remarks make you a welcome guest, as you can be counted on to blend into the group and also provide fresh ideas.

You are not one to do the dirty work. Perhaps you don't want to get stains on your nice clothes or get dirt under your fingernails. You can be seen as overly refined if you refuse to do what it takes to clean up the messes that are created in the course of living. However, you can—and do—indulge yourself with the best tools available when a task is unpleasant. You may keep a supply of disposable rubber gloves so that the icky stuff never touches your hands, and you may have several aprons of different styles to keep you looking good when you are cooking.

You very much enjoy the accolades for a successful party, a well-directed meeting, or an enjoyable backyard croquet game. When it is your turn, you dish out compliments, too. You have a knack for focusing your compliments on the area where the other person has obviously invested personal effort, and then saying why and how that effort has been successful. You know that praise works best when it goes both ways.

Ascendant in Scorpio

The Scorpio Ascendant thrives in an aggressive environment. You are able to fight life-and-death battles, whether real or metaphorical, with style and determination. If life is too placid, too easy, you look for ways to increase the urgency. This means that you are stressed a lot, and you may create stress for others through unnecessary agitation. You are a good person to have around in a crisis, as you have developed crisis management to the nth degree.

A large part of your sexual magnetism is actually driven by an instinctual desire to procreate. You enjoy wild passion, too, but it is the desire for children that fuels your intense magnetic attraction. Both sexes marvel at the energy that radiates from you. They are almost certainly more timid in this area than you, and they may believe you are much more active sexually than you are.

Under your very assertive exterior, there is a reserved, rather cautious person. You are ready for action, but it is because you have prepared yourself with a lifetime of thought and practice, as well as research into the current situation. You are the metaphorical emergency medical technician who has the proper equipment and training to handle the blood and gore. You can make quick decisions when you have to.

Ascendant in Sagittarius

Sagittarius is mutable fire. This is a very sensible combination when you think about it. Fire goes where it finds fuel, ebbing and flowing with the breeze. With Sagittarius rising, you follow this metaphor in everything you do. You can expand when that is needed, and contract as well. You can aspire to spiritual heights, or get down to the nitty-gritty of a project. You enjoy being around other people.

Because you have lofty thoughts and goals, you desire appropriate recognition for your work. You are plenty smart, but you are not satisfied to be the brains behind a big production—you want your name on it. By the same token, you like to run with a pack that is at your level. Thus you cultivate long-term relationships with your peers and gain a reputation for fairness and consistency.

You love to be outdoors. You are a rugged individual and may take up cross-country hiking or skiing, camping, and other activities that bring you into contact with nature. You enjoy an adventure, and therefore plan vacations that take you to untamed parts of the world. Your spirit needs the open air in order to expand to its full potential, so outdoor activities are vital to your overall well-being.

Ascendant in Capricorn

Perhaps the most self-controlled Ascendant sign, Capricorn sometimes comes across as being more rigid than the fixed signs, even though it is in the active mode. Your persona is laced all around with responsibility and concentration, two worthy attributes of Saturn, the planet associated with this sign. People learn to depend on you, even though you may be gruff or abrupt in demeanor. You have the seal of reliability.

You are self-directed. You come up with the game plan, and you refine the practical aspects so that it plays out well. You generally play by the rules. The catch is, you also make up the rules. This works well as long as other people are willing to go along. There may be times when your ideas clash with the people around you in startling ways.

For all your will and direction, you may come across as rather shy. Perhaps you have had the experience of overpowering others, and you don't want to do that again. Or perhaps you feel the weight of responsibility and don't want to add sociability to that burden. When you are among people who you know well, you come out of your cave and can be a lot of fun.

Ascendant in Aquarius

You surround yourself with people and circumstances that favor changing the world. Your persona lends itself to reforming, as you are open to new ideas, willing to escape the confines of older restrictions, and generally able to guide the process of change skillfully. While you sometimes feel rebellious, you usually come across as innovative rather than destructive.

You have a fundamental understanding of human nature that enables you to gain the cooperation of people around you. You appreciate the ideas of others and incorporate them with your own in any venture. Your broad interests are reflected in your ability to participate in discussions on a wide range of topics, and you are capable of changing your objectives to suit the situation.

Whether you show it to others or not, you have a deep connection to the universe. Your spiritual beliefs may be quite different from your family and contemporaries, and yet you retain the core values you were taught as a child to a large extent. You just frame them differently than your parents did.

Ascendant in Pisces

It is really hard for others to get to know you. It's not that you are super secretive, although you don't reveal much. Rather, your natural reserve comes across as shyness or as an unwillingness to engage with your environment.

You can become lonely and depressed because you don't reach out to others easily. Your may give off a vibe that says, "Leave me alone," and then you are alone and lonely. While this is not the desired outcome, it is comfortable in its own way. You don't have to make the effort to spend time with other people, and you can retire to the comfort of your own "nest."

Inside, you are filled with a wealth of feelings. You may be naturally empathic, feeling what everyone else is feeling most of the time. You probably think your feelings are just as evident to others, but this is simply not the case. If you want others to understand where you are coming from, you have to express your feelings in words and action.

Case Study: Henri Toulouse-Lautrec

Henri Toulouse-Lautrec was a French post-Impressionist artist who was famous for both painting and printmaking. One of his most famous paintings is "At the Moulin Rouge." He also painted numerous portraits and scenes from daily life in Paris. Lautrec had Scorpio on the Ascendant. We can consider what we know about Scorpio and use this to identify his persona—how he presented himself to the world.

Sex is one of the first associations most people make with the sign of Scorpio. Lautrec was no slouch in this department. In spite of his numerous physical limitations, which will be discussed in the chapter about Mars (chapter 8), Lautrec had plenty of female friends, and he spent plenty of time with them in their beds. He understood the compelling power of sexual attraction. His art demonstrates that he perceived the power inherent in physical relationships.

Lautrec was a person of strong desires. He wanted to have friends, and he wanted them to do his bidding. Historical data indicate that he drove himself where his art was concerned, and when he was not working on it, he was applying himself to the study of human nature.

He was jealous of his mother. When she left him as a young child for a two-month period, he was devastated. He needed her to be around him, and as an adult he had dinner with her several times a week. Toward the end of his life, when he was suffering from the effects of alcoholism and other excesses, she deserted him. This undoubtedly contributed to his rapid decline and death.

Thus we see that Lautrec had the constructive traits of penetrating intellect and determination, coupled with desires that went to excess, somewhat degenerate sexual interests, and a profoundly creative artistic ability.

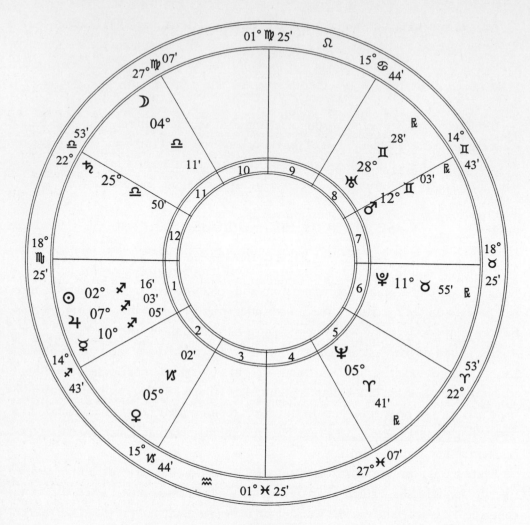

Chart 10
Henri Toulouse-Lautrec
November 24, 1864 / Albi, France / 6:00 A.M. LMT
Koch Houses

The Sun, Moon, and Ascendant Describe the Personality

So far you have read a bit about the planets signs, houses, and aspects in general. You have also met the Sun, Moon, and Ascendant. These three points in the chart describe your basic personality. The Sun is who you are—your individuality. The Moon reflects your hidden, subconscious tendencies, as well as your private thoughts. The Ascendant is what you choose to show to the world, and as a result, how you tend to see the world around you.

With just these three parts of the chart, you can begin to learn about yourself or another person through the birthchart. We still have the planets and the Midheaven to consider, so the picture will become far more complex, but with these three components you can reveal a great deal about an individual.

More about Toulouse-Lautrec

Henri had the Sun in Sagittarius and the Moon in Libra. Let's look at how these three placements describe his overall personality.

With the Sun in Sagittarius, Henri was deeply intuitive. He saw into the lives of people around him, and this insight was reflected in his art. He was not afraid to use color and shape to evoke a feeling about his subjects. He had powerful relationships with people and was able to form lasting friendships despite his odd appearance, his physical limitations, and his alcoholic behavior. To a large extent this was due to his ability to have fun.

The Libra Moon suggests a profound desire for balance and harmony. Henri was fully capable of expressing his desires, as his letters demonstrate. He expressed the desire to be close to his mother and to his friends—he craved social activity. Some irresponsibility is indicated, and Henri certainly fulfilled this promise in his chart through partying and drunkenness.

The Scorpio Ascendant is able to apply pressure to both the Sagittarius Sun and the Libra Moon. Henri was a formidable figure despite his short stature. He had a dark appearance that reflected a dark emotional interior. At the same time he had the ability to engage in relationships that went beyond the surface social niceties. He used his ability to see into the lives of other people to enhance his art.

Exercise

Using your chart (or someone else's chart), write down three things about each point: the Sun, Moon, and Ascendant. Be sure to seek a balance between your positive and less constructive traits.

1. Using a colored marker, circle or highlight the things on your list that feel consistent with each other.

2. Using a second color, underline those things on your list that seem antithetical to each other.

3. Think of ways that the consistent items can support the antithetical ones. How can you use your individuality, for example, to overcome a limitation of your Moon? How does a quality of your Ascendant help balance a less desirable Sun-sign quality?

Do you feel you need to change anything to get the Sun, Moon, and Ascendant to work better together? Can you make such a change? Perhaps you see that they work well together. What can you do to enhance the most positive side of your personality?

Summary

The planets move relatively slowly, and their positions in the zodiac on any given day can be found in a listing called an *ephemeris*. (There is an example of an ephemeris in chapter 14.) The Ascendant moves much faster than the planets, going through the entire zodiac each day. Its calculation depends on a precise birth time. If your time of birth is unknown, you can work with a chart that places the Sun at either the Ascendant or Midheaven. If at the Ascendant, it will be as though you were born at sunrise, and if at the Midheaven, you might have been born at noon. With no birth time, you will not be able to determine your Ascendant and house cusps, except through investigation of events. This process, called rectification, is beyond the scope of this book. Even without the Ascendant, your exploration of the planets and their aspects can be very helpful in understanding yourself and how you function in the world. In the next chapter, we will consider Mercury, the planet of communication.

---

1. Noel Tyl, *Synthesis and Counseling in Astrology* (St. Paul, Minn.: Llewellyn Publications, 1998) 69.

2. Kevin Burk, *Astrology: Understanding the Birth Chart* (St. Paul, Minn.: Llewellyn Publications, 2001) 176.

3. Gail Fairfield, *Choice Centered Astrology* (York Beach, Maine: Weiser, 1998) 247.

4. Alice Bailey, *Esoteric Astrology* (New York: Lucis Publishing, 1979) 17.

6

Mercury, the Third and Sixth Houses, and the Trine

Throughout mythology, Mercury, in his Greek and other cultural guises, was messenger to the gods. This association with words and communication pervades the literature of religion and myth. In the Old Testament (Genesis 1:3), God said, "Let there be light." In the New Testament (John 1:1), John states, "In the beginning was the Word, and the Word was with God, and the Word was God." In these quotations, communicating through words precedes ordinary existence. It is certain that before there was verbal language, human communication was extremely primitive. The capacity for deductive reasoning depends on language.

Buddhism teaches that one area of knowledge is learning the names of things. Through learning the names and the characteristics associated with things, we learn to relate to the world in ways that are consistent with social norms. We also learn to make sense of the complex world of physical, mental, emotional, and spiritual things, events, and concepts.

Mercury is androgynous. It is neither masculine nor feminine in itself, but takes on the qualities of the sign and house it occupies, and the qualities of planets it connects to through aspects. This is totally appropriate for the messenger. It carries the message without judging its content. This means that Mercury's sign can be seen clearly in your personality through the words you choose. Your speech will be strongly colored by this sign, and by Mercury's relationship to other planets.

Mercury indicates what we have learned through the vehicle of communication. Thus Mercury also shows how our minds are organized. We assimilate information via the Moon—the Moon represents all kinds of nurturing. Once information has gone into the mind, several things can happen. Generally information is stored. Some of this storage is orderly memory, with systematic means of retrieval. Some information is basically forgotten. It may reside in memory, but there is no ready means of recovering it. Something may remind us of what we know, but otherwise those thoughts will not arise. Finally, we sometimes repress or suppress memories of all kinds when they are unacceptable or unpleasant. Those particular memories are actively submerged in the unconscious, and we use psychological energy to keep from recalling them.

Because Mercury is the messenger, this planet indicates how we bring ideas together. Mediation can be between social factions, or it can be between psychological positions within our own minds. The concept of mediation hinges on the possibility that we experience conflict, and that we can achieve harmony by engaging in conflict in a meaningful way. If we can perceive or establish communication among the parties, we can usually find the middle ground. Diplomacy is paired with intellectual skills of analysis and awareness to reach some level of agreement.

The root of Mercury's function is truth. From the strength of God's word (and this is true in all world religions), to the power of intellect and communication in social circumstances, to the awareness and will of individual minds, we thrive on the truth and seek it out. We develop critical-thinking skills to analyze data, and we devise research methods to discover truth in just about every area of experience.

Mercury Through the Signs

Mercury in Aries

Intellect and intuition meet in a synergistic way with Mercury in Aries. Your ability to observe and analyze situations is enhanced by your ability to foresee events and outcomes. In writing and other communications, you have a quick wit that engages your audience. You sometimes overwork yourself because you try to follow every mental impulse and therefore never seem to get enough rest. You even do problem-solving in your sleep!

Mercury in Taurus

Your logical mind is more methodical in its process than Mercury in Aries. You have the patience to follow a thought along its meandering path, and you want to see the end result. Although you are patient in discovering and refining your own ideas, you sometimes end up with only one side of a broader picture. Then you stubbornly hold on to your view, unwilling to even consider another perspective.

Mercury in Gemini

Your thought processes are very clear and very versatile. You consider a number of perspectives, and you quantify and qualify differences with ease. You enjoy change so much that you even change your mind about major issues in your life. You then come across as inconsistent or, worse, dishonest. Yes, you have a right to change your mind. And you are well placed in a career that provides constant change to keep you interested.

Mercury in Cancer

Your mental gift is to connect the logical thinking process with the feeling process. Normally people are strong in one or the other, but you can bring them together. The advantage is that you can think through a problem logically, and then make a judgment about how each potential outcome will look and feel, before you make your decision. You become totally focused on tasks, to the point where you lose track of your surroundings.

Mercury in Leo

Your enthusiasm is easily communicated to others, and motivation is one of your most potent leadership skills. You can see far down the road to the desired result, and then backtrack to figure out how to get there from here. At your best, you are able to provide constructive advice or criticism to coworkers and employees. You are a great organizer, and people learn to trust your judgment. All the while, you have your personal creative projects percolating, so you seem to get twice as much done as most people.

Mercury in Virgo

Your thirst for knowledge finds you reading one more book or taking one more class all the time. You are not satisfied until you master a subject, and you may become known for your expertise in more than one arena. Your orderly mental style is reflected in your environment, and you may become nervous when things are too messy. You are a team player and contribute your fair share of effort to projects.

Mercury in Libra

You are able to take a system of thought or a group of ideas and work within the set boundaries. As you do this, you apply your thoughts to how to "work" the system. You are able to compare very different sets of information to find the commonalities. Your social skills are obvious in tactful conversation, and you may even be a skilled mediator. Because you can see more than one side of a situation, you are a valuable team player.

Mercury in Scorpio

You have sharpened your tongue and can do battle with the best of them, but don't expect to be friends afterward. They may respect you, but they won't want to get cozy. Yet you will be the first person they come to when they need someone on their side because you tell it like it is, without any window dressing. Your skepticism helps you see past the surface details to the deeper issues.

Mercury in Sagittarius

A deeply religious tendency underlies your mental processes. Philosophical leanings color your life. At the same time there is a tendency to scatter your energy, exploring many interests but often not completing your search. Sometimes you try to take the easier path to avoid confrontation. There is an abiding appreciation for the truth. You seek to solve or resolve life's problems. You tend to speak what is on your mind, even though it may be inconvenient.

Mercury in Capricorn

Your powers of mental concentration are superior. You can solve the most difficult problems because you focus, use logic, and keep the end goal in mind. You are shrewd in business dealings, and do the necessary homework before you dedicate your resources to any purchase or project. When you are too consumed with mental tasks, you can become rather gloomy, and you need to give yourself regular breaks—walk around the block to air out your mind from time to time.

Mercury in Aquarius

Your naturally quick Mercury thrives in Aquarius because planning uses the problem-solving capacity of your mind. You are quick on the uptake, seeing any problem for what it is—a puzzle to be solved. While you prefer to work alone, coming to your own solution, others like to have you on their team because they admire your results. You could be an inventor, as you have original ideas about how things work.

Mercury in Pisces

You are rather easily swayed by other people. Knowing this, you have an advantage. You can be your usual compliant self, reserving your decision until you have all the information. You will find that other people expect you to go along with them all the time, but you don't have to. Practice saying the word "No" in front of a mirror if you have to. That way you can say it when the chips are down.

The Third House—Home of Mercury and Verbal Communication

The planet Mercury is associated with two signs—Gemini and Virgo—and thus it is also associated with two houses—the Third and the Sixth. The Third House describes matters often associated with childhood. Education is a key factor, with school environment and short-distance travel part of the educational process. Siblings are shown here, as are neighbors. Communication through reading, writing, telephone, email, and other means is read through this house. Overall the Third House indicates how you express yourself to others, and also how you think.

The physical associations with the Third House include the arms, wrists, and fingers. In addition the shoulders, lungs, and thyroid gland are reflected here. The nervous system and the emotional "nerve" of the person are Third House considerations. Because hearing and speech are integral to communication, indicators of any problems or exceptional skills are connected to this house. The nervous system is essential for motor activity of all kinds, and especially for writing, sculpture, painting, and verbal communication. Healthy thyroid function is essential for normal physical and mental development in children, and continues to be important for healthy metabolism throughout life.

In summary, the Third House reveals mental and physical development in childhood, as well as early education and communication skill. It also addresses the impact of siblings, neighbors, and neighborhood in the individual. Finally, the Third House indicates the thyroid, shoulders, arms, finger, wrists, and lungs, and their general function.

The Sixth House—Home of Mercury and Communication Through Work

The Sixth House relates to general health indications, to the work environment, and to work in general. The distinction between the Third and Sixth Houses is made largely on the basis of a mental/verbal focus versus a physical focus. Although this is not entirely true, it is a useful way to think of the differences between what is essentially an air house and an earth house.

The Sixth House is associated with the diaphragm, intestines, solar plexus, and bowels. Mercury is the planet associated with breath, as breath is essential for verbal communication. The Third House is associated with the lungs, and the Sixth with the diaphragm, the muscle that controls breath. Diet, digestion, and assimilation are essential to health, and the Sixth House indicates the overall condition of the digestive organs.

The Sixth House reflects the work environment and relationships with co-workers. How you provide service to others is also shown here. The Sixth House is not so much about career (seen in the Tenth House), but about the actual place you work. This house describes the building, office space, geographical location, direction the windows face, etc. It also describes co-workers, if any, and other relationships within the work environment. It indicates roles both of service and servant. The sign reflects the primary work functions that are most advantageous for you.

How Planets Function in Different Signs

In the chapter on the Sun, we discussed the elements (fire, earth, air, and water) and the qualities, or modes (cardinal, fixed, and mutable) in relation to the twelve signs of the zodiac. We also talked about the Moon, Ascendant, and Venus and how they function in different signs. We saw how each sign expresses one element and one mode.

In addition to the element and mode of each sign, traditional astrology assigns alternating roles to the signs in order through the zodiac. The first role is assertive and direct, while the second is receptive and responsive. These are often described as being *mascu-*

line or *feminine* in nature, although these terms have come to be less meaningful in contemporary society where gender roles have become somewhat blurred. The fire and air signs are generally more assertive, while earth and water signs are more receptive.

What does this mean in terms of your chart? When planets are found in assertive signs, they are somewhat more able to express themselves. Receptive signs indicate planetary energies that may be reflected in more cautious expression, or that tend to respond to circumstances instead of creating them. The rhythm of assertion and receptivity is to move from one to the other. Neither is static. You are never all one or the other. Thus the movement from one sign to the next incorporates the rhythm of expression/response.

What happens when a planet is found in a responsive sign? The planet's energy is experienced in a modified way. The same is true for a planet in an expressive sign. Think of a stage filled with players. To be effective, the drama must move from active scenes to more passive moments, from tragedy to humor, from major events to quiet, introspective interludes. Otherwise we could not understand the characters and the story. A slightly more sympathetic Hamlet might have encouraged Ophelia's interest in him, and a slightly more assertive Ophelia might have survived to help Hamlet gain his revenge. Their actions reveal the stark contrast of their characters.

Traditional Planet/Sign Compatibility

As children we learn to moderate the energies within us, as indicated by our birthchart. If we don't manage this, we are faced over and over again with difficult lessons. A planet's energy flows better when it is in a compatible sign, and it reflects more of a struggle when in a less compatible sign. Here are some traditional astrological ideas about planets and the signs where they are most powerful.

Sign Ruler

The word *ruler* is used to designate the sign in which a planet naturally belongs. This is a very comfortable place for the planet and is called its domicile, or home.

Sign of Detriment

This sign is opposite the domicile. By *detriment*, astrologers mean that you have to work harder to express this planet's energy well. Because of the extra work, in the end we often master this energy and it becomes part of our group of well-developed skills.

Sign of Exaltation

The dictionary definition of the term *exaltation* indicates an intensified sense of well-being or power. The energy of a planet in its exaltation, then, is amplified and free to operate more powerfully.

Sign Where a Planet "Falls"

When a planet is in fall, there is a loss of greatness. The energy of the planet is not initially able to express its full potential. The energy is there, but needs to be cultivated. It's like having a fabulous car with flat tires. Something needs to "pump up" a planet in fall. This is not as difficult to do as when the planet is in detriment, where significant work is needed to master the energy. But it does require help from elsewhere in the chart.

The following table indicates the traditional signs of compatibility (called *dignity*). Modern astrologers include Uranus, Neptune, and Pluto in this scheme, even though these planets were unknown when the system of rulerships was first developed. Each planet has only one sign of exaltation and fall, and therefore some of the signs have been left blank. In addition, the assertive and receptive sign are indicated by + and –.

Exercise

Consider the sign placement of each planet in your chart.

1. Identify planets in their own sign.
2. Identify planets in signs of detriment, exaltation, or fall.
3. Identify which planets are in positive and negative signs.
4. Which planets seem to be the most comfortable?
5. Which planets are in uncomfortable signs?

Based on your responses, try to think of ways you could work with the energies of the strong planets to support the weaker ones. As you read the following chapters, see if you discover ideas about how to balance the planets so that the weaker ones are strengthened and supported.

Sign		Ruler	Detriment (opposite rulership)	Exaltation*	Fall (opposite exaltation)
Aries	+	Mars	Venus	Sun	Saturn
Taurus	–	Venus	Mars (Pluto)	Moon	
Gemini	+	Mercury	Jupiter	North Node	South Node
Cancer	–	Moon	Saturn	Jupiter	Mars
Leo	+	Sun	Saturn (Uranus)		
Virgo	–	Mercury	Jupiter (Neptune)	Mercury	Venus
Libra	+	Venus	Mars	Saturn	Sun
Scorpio	–	Mars (Pluto)	Venus		Moon
Sagittarius	+	Jupiter	Mercury	South Node	North Node
Capricorn	–	Saturn	Moon	Mars	Jupiter
Aquarius	+	Saturn (Uranus)	Sun		
Pisces	–	Jupiter (Neptune)	Mercury	Venus	Mercury

---

* This table indicates the dignities according to Ptolemy, an astrologer who lived between approximately 87 and 150 C.E. The planets in parentheses indicate rulerships for the more recently discovered outer planets.

Chart 11
Essential Dignities and Debilities

The Trine Aspect

The trine represents the third harmonic, or 360/3. Recall the earlier description of the elements and modes. Planets in trine to each other are generally in signs of the same element (planets in the same mode are square and will be covered in the next chapter). When planets are in the same element, they are able to function smoothly together because they share the same psychological function and other qualities. Planets in fire signs are intuitive and relate comfortably with each other through that medium. Earth signs share the sensation function, air signs share thinking, and water signs share the capacity for feeling.

When planets are in this kind of comfortable relationship, they work together naturally. In fact they work together without any particular effort on your part. You come to expect the easy relationship, and you may even become lazy where these energies are concerned precisely because they are so easy and natural. Thus trines have two sides: On the one hand they are comfortable and consistent. On the other hand, they don't stimulate your mind, and therefore you aren't challenged to learn how to use the energies indicated by the aspecting planets.

Often we only learn to take advantage of the energy reflected in trines because we are also experiencing other aspects. When a planet in the heavens today (a *transiting* planet[1]) arrives at the same degree as one of your birth planets, they form a conjunction, and both planets are highlighted. We can observe the beginning or ending of some comfortable condition—comfortable because the aspect in the birthchart is a trine, and beginning or ending because the transiting planet forms a conjunction. If a transiting planet forms some other aspect, this indicates a different kind of interaction about an area of your life that has usually been comfortable. You perceive the mechanism that provides for comfort in different ways. In the following chapters you will learn more about the other aspects. As you learn about them, you will see how they interact with each other in your chart to form familiar patterns of behavior.

When working with trines, remember that you have free will. Whatever condition you experience, desirable or not so desirable, you have the capacity to work with it. You can enhance pleasant conditions and learn to recall them at will. You can examine unpleasant conditions and learn to bring them to resolution. The easiest way to do either is to work with the energy of the element the planets occupy. Let's review what you have learned about the elements with this in mind.

- For planets in fire signs, you will want to listen to your intuition to find the best solution for any problem involved in the trine aspect. You can also use your intuition to see possible future ways to maintain or restore the comfortable energetic relationship represented by the aspect.

- For planets in earth signs, your approach will be largely practical. You will consider adjustments or changes on the material level. For example, you may move furniture and materials around for easier access.

- For planets in air signs, you may want to communicate with the people around you concerning your perceptions and desires. You will also want to find ways to listen to your own internal voice of reason.

- For planets in water signs, you will often have a gut reaction to situations and feel your way through changes in that way. You will exercise judgment: Is this pleasant or unpleasant? Do I like the way this is going?

Case Study: Muhammad Ali

Muhammad Ali provides a wonderful example of trines in action. He has many trines, including Sun-Uranus, Sun-Saturn, Uranus-Neptune, Saturn-Neptune, Neptune-Sun, Moon-Jupiter, and Mercury-Jupiter. The Sun, Uranus, and Neptune are each in an earth sign and form a Grand Trine—a triangle of trines.

Too often Grand Trines reflect a life of such ease that the individual comes to expect—even demand—the goodies. Such a person becomes lazy and may even turn to illegal activities as the easiest way to get what he or she wants. Ali avoided many of the pitfalls of this comfortable pattern. At age twelve he experienced the world of boxing for the first time, and his career was set. Unlike other fighters who got into trouble on the street, Ali restricted his fighting to the ring.

His birthchart indicates that Ali's trines were supported by other aspects. Mars, the planet of aggression, forms a square to his Sun. As you will see in chapter 8, this square provides a challenge or push to the otherwise lazy Grand Trine. A square involving Venus and Saturn provides a stabilizing influence as well.

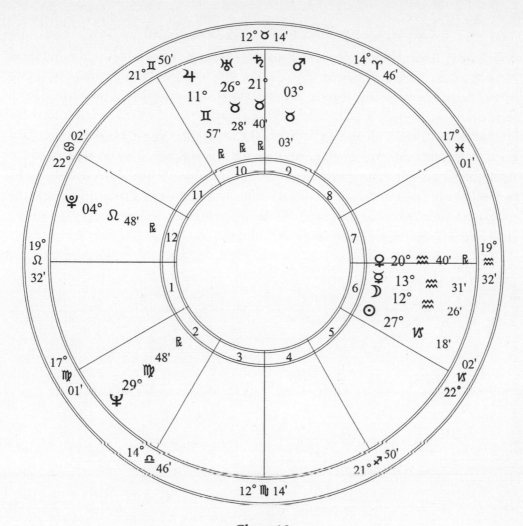

Chart 12

Muhammad Ali

January 17, 1942 / Louisville, KY / 6:35 P.M. CST

Koch Houses

Case Study: His Holiness the Dalai Lama

A contrast to Ali in almost every way, the Dalai Lama also has a Grand Trine, but his is in water signs. The Sun in Cancer trines Jupiter in Scorpio and Saturn in Pisces. (Pluto is too far from these three planets to form trines.) His Grand Trine is also "pushed" by a square from Mars to the Sun. The water planets speak to the depth of compassion in his life, and Mars in Libra, an air sign, indicates the mode through which he has mobilized his energy—the thinking function. Both Ali and His Holiness have demonstrated the strength of their spiritual convictions. While the spiritual life would not necessarily be part of one's life as seen through trines, it is often true that we find spiritual value in the simple comforts we discover in life. Both Ali and His Holiness have fought to care for and preserve something of their respective cultures.

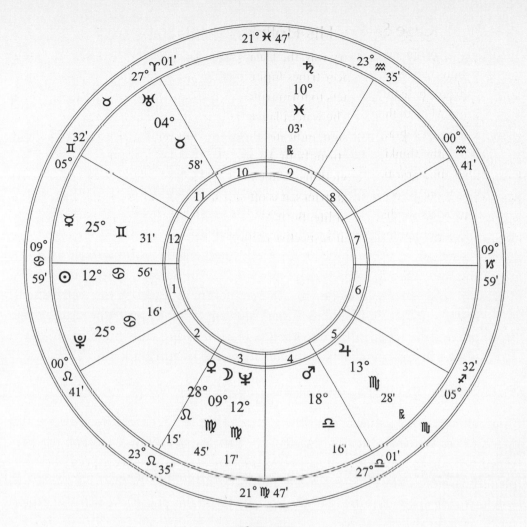

Chart 13
His Holiness the Dalai Lama
July 6, 1935 / Tengster Village, Tibet
101E12 36N32 / 4:38 A.M. LMT
Koch Houses

Exercise

Look at your own chart and see if you have any trine aspects.

1. If you have trines, look at the signs and the element involved. How does this element function in your life? What can you do to increase or amplify this potential source of comfort?

2. If the planets are in different elements, you still may have trines. For example, a planet at 28 degrees Aries forms trines to planets at 2 degrees Virgo and 3 degrees Capricorn. Think about what it means to have an otherwise comfortable aspect that involves two elements. Your trine may not be quite so comfortable. What can you do to get the energies to work together?

3. If you have no trines, this does not mean you cannot have comfortable areas of your life. When the planets move forward, they form trines. When this happens, what can you consciously do to create comfort in your life? As you read the section about squares, for example, you may want to think about how the challenge of the square can develop into a source of comfort and satisfaction, as one of the planets in the square moves forward 30 degrees to form a trine.

Summary

Communication is essential to a healthy, successful life. In this chapter you have seen the specific roles of Mercury in each sign, and you have learned about the two houses associated with this planet. The trine aspect was introduced, as it is the aspect where two planets have especially good communication with each other. In the next chapter, we will look at Venus and the two houses associated with this planet. We will also explore the opposition aspect.

---

1. See chapter 14 on transits for more information.

7

Venus, the Second and Seventh Houses, and the Opposition

The similarities between the Earth and Venus are as striking as the differences. From the astronomical perspective, here are some facts: Venus is close to the size of the Earth (86 percent of the Earth's volume and 93 percent of its gravity). Overall Venus has slightly less density as well. Its axial inclination is 178 degrees, compared to the Earth's 23.5 degrees. Venus is a nearly perfect sphere and has a nearly perfect circular orbit. Because Venus is between the Earth and Sun, phases similar to those of the Moon are observable. Because of its atmosphere, a halo is visible at the time of the inferior conjunction (when Venus is between the Sun and Earth).

Now for the striking differences. The rotation of Venus on its axis is longer than its revolution around the Sun—243.2 days compared to 224.7 days. Venus is the only planet where this occurs. Venus rotates from east to west, the opposite of the Earth. The atmosphere is mostly carbon dioxide, with a lot of sulfur dioxide and sulfuric acid. The atmosphere has a vastly shorter rotational period than the planet itself. High-altitude clouds rotate in only four days! The surface temperature is around 500 degrees centigrade, and the surface pressure is about 90 atmospheres, or 90 times as much pressure as we experience on Earth. The conditions can be likened to our conceptualizations of Hell.

Some astrologers have characterized Venus as the alter ego of the Earth. In Aztec mythology, Quetzalcoatl was Venus as the morning star, and his sinister sister Xolotl was Venus as the evening star. He was the herald of the Sun, while she was the bringer of darkness. Xolotl was a horrifying figure. Considering what we know about Venus' physical attributes, and what we know about our concept of the alter ego, this actually makes sense. If we take the alter ego to be the opposite side of our personality—the less conscious side—then we assign to it the unpleasant attributes of personality—sort of a Jekyll and Hyde relationship.

If we look at another meaning of alter ego—that of trusted friend—we find two possibilities. First, the trusted friend can be another person. The social attributes associated with Venus in the astrological chart are consistent with this view. Venus' house is opposite the Ascendant in the chart. The Ascendant and the First House represent your own persona, while the Seventh House represents the persona of your significant others—romantic and business partners, as well as anyone who is significant in your life. Often the trusted friend is a person who is able to state strong opinions about you without hurting your feelings. Such a person is a sort of barometer of your moral, emotional, psychological, and even spiritual character.

Secondly, the unconscious component of personality can achieve a similar position of trust. As we grow and learn, we become more familiar with the inner world of the unconscious mind. Dreams provide us with information about our unconscious life. We go through periods of self-doubt, and we question the validity of suppressing parts of our personalities. In therapy we take a long hard look at less conscious material. In short, we become familiar with it—we make friends with it. As we release thoughts and feelings from the unconscious, we enjoy a more harmonious life of joy and contentment. These are qualities sometimes associated with Venus.

The role of Venus in the astrological chart is to reveal the qualities of love, harmony, and art in our lives. Venus indicates the way we experience physical attraction. We are drawn to something outside ourselves. And it is through such attractions that we experience the richness of living. Venus shows how and where we can cultivate a positive attitude. Venus reflects impressionability. We hope to be appreciative of others without giving in to their demands too easily. We seek companions who reinforce our best qualities and help us correct our weaknesses. We are better off when we display charm and devotion appropriately, instead of demonstrating vanity and jealousy.

Throughout all these qualities, the theme of harmony is expressed again and again. Venus by its sign, house, and aspects indicates the general state of harmony in the birthchart. Venus also indicates the kinds of relationships that attract our attention and effort most easily. I find that Venus indicates what is "nice" in my life. "Nice" is a very subjective term. Therefore we must keep in mind that Venus means something different for each of us. This planet may seem to take on very different roles in different charts— roles suggestive of the alter ego of the individual or event.

Three Expressions of the Feminine

Venus is considered to be a feminine planet, although it is associated with one feminine sign, Taurus, and one masculine sign, Libra. Throughout literature we find three distinctly different expressions of the feminine: the Lover, the Companion, and the Seeker.

- The Lover is exemplified by Venus and Aphrodite, her Greek counterpart. Aphrodite is said to have been birthed from the sea when Ouranus' blood mingled with Neptune's waters. Her beauty and charms attracted many suitors, among them Ares, with whom she had two sons, Phobos and Deimos. Isis, the Egyptian counterpart, was wife of Osiris and mother to Horus. Venus as lover represents all the magic of physical and sexual attraction. Desire is not inherently bad. However, taken to the extreme it can become a vice. Moderation was not a theme associated with Aphrodite.

- The Companion has a different partnership role. Venus reflects the friendship in this kind of relationship, which may also be part of the passionate-desire relationship. Some of the best romantic relationships begin as friendship and grow into a more profound connection. Selected attributes of Venus in the astrological chart include consideration, cooperation, and companionship. This side of Venus incorporates sociable, courteous qualities that are the essence of this type of relationship.

- The Seeker of Knowledge is a third expression of Venus. Esoteric traditions indicate that Venus is associated with concrete knowledge, and several myths cast Venus in the role of seeker. For example, her Sumerian counterpart is Inanna. Inanna sought rulership of the temple of Anu, and in order to achieve this position, she went to her Uncle Enki. After extended partying, Enki became drunk and told Inanna she could have anything she wanted. She asked for the knowledge that would make civilization possible, and Enki came through with information regarding the roles of kings and priests, the use of weapons, legal matters, wood-working, and even the knowledge of musical instruments (music in the astrological chart is indicated by Venus).

If you are interested in an in-depth study of Venus/Aphrodite or other mythology associated with astrology, see the recommended reading in the bibliography on goddesses. I encourage you to see Venus as a multifaceted energy in your chart. Venusian interactions often incorporate more than one of these expressions, and may also include a warrior aspect as well.

Venus Through the Signs

Venus in Aries

Venus in Aries has strong creative powers. The power is there naturally, but the method must be acquired through personal effort. You try several creative and artistic ventures, and you may push the limits of each artistic form you encounter, always searching for the best expression of your feelings in the moment.

You can fall in love at first sight, and you may do so more than once in your life. Love is viewed as an adventure, and you always like a new romance if the old one loses its excitement. This does not make you the ideal partner, as your sense of commitment is not as strong as your desire for adventure. You can have a long-term relationship, but it will depend on other factors in your chart.

Venus in Taurus

You relish the long-term relationship—one where you can put down roots and grow into it steadfastly. Your strong powers of attraction make getting into partnerships easy. The task is to determine who is the right partner, whether in business or romance, before you make a commitment you will be unwilling to dissolve.

Your artistic talents may include making jewelry or sculpting stone. You understand whatever artistic medium you use—the consistency of the paint, the depth of tone in a musical instrument, the shapes of words on the page. And you stick with each project or medium, seeking to discover the beauty within each form. This method of pursuit extends to all your dealings, artistic or otherwise.

Venus in Gemini

You have the voice to be very convincing. You may be a powerful speaker, or you may develop singing talent. Others enjoy listening to you, and they also enjoy listening to your work performed by others. Writing is a talent you can cultivate throughout your life.

Your charming personality gets you invited into many social circles, as you always fit in with the crowd. You enjoy discussing your ideas with others, and you are also a good listener.

You can appear superficial simply because of the breadth of your interests. In many cases your interest does skim the surface. However, you are constantly developing bridges from one subject to the next, drawing parallels and finding contrasts. Eventually you find one or two subjects that hold your interest, and these you understand on every level—physical, mental, emotional, and spiritual.

Venus in Cancer

Love runs very deep within you, and you expect the same from your partner. You believe you should be able to depend on your significant other to be supportive and to share an interest in family. You may have wanted to bring your friends home and have them live with you when you were younger, and were dismayed when they wanted to go back to their own families.

You enjoy good food and occasionally suffer from overindulgence. Dietary and nutritional moderation will be reflected by other planets in your chart. By the same token, you can put together wonderful parties and meals, making the setting sparkle and ensuring that the food is attractive and delicious.

Venus in Leo

You enjoy living well. You begin with yourself, choosing your clothing carefully so that you always look elegant and refined. Then you address your home with the same attention to detail. In the process you can spend a lot of money, but your expensive tastes stand the test of time, as your selections don't go out of style and they fit together into a unified theme.

You enjoy the social circuit and attract romantic partners easily. Because of your deep feelings, you may jump into marriage or a long-term commitment prematurely. You very much enjoy the game, so a permanent relationship will require a partner who likes to play. One of you has to take care of the business of your relationship if it is to be successful.

Venus in Virgo

You have a sense of propriety and ethics that carries into all your relationships. External considerations may interfere with romance, as you are paying more attention to your social position than to your partner. However, this strength of character can mold you into a desirable mate. You see your partnership as a team effort, and you unselfishly consider the interests of both parties.

Initially you may be indecisive about partners of all kinds. This keeps you out of messy alliances, but it also delays the development of lasting associations. You have to strike a balance between your desire for perfection and your desire for a partner, as no one is likely to measure up to your highest standards all the time.

Venus in Libra

You are naturally friendly and obliging, and this makes some people think you are a pushover. You're not. You have a knack for being agreeable while all the time thinking your own thoughts and making your own plans. You are a networker of the first order, always finding connections between people and things. Naturally, all this activity keeps you very busy.

Because you are so busy, you scatter your energy and therefore may not have time for a serious relationship. If your partners become irritated because you are off doing other stuff and ignoring them, you should take their complaints seriously. If you want that long-term relationship, you have to put in your 50 percent (or more) to make it work. Maybe you can find activities that you can do together—teamwork and equal partnership.

Venus in Scorpio

Your powers of attraction baffle others of your sex. You may not be the best looking, the richest, or the most congenial, but you are sought after because of your animal magnetism. And you are a passionate being. You can go overboard with extremes—aberrant sexual behavior or multiple, frequent partners. Or you may be just the opposite. You may be delicate or even prudish in your sexual appetites. After all, sex is a private activity, right?

Your passions run to other things besides sex. You can waste your time and energy jumping into activities without testing the water first. You are in over your head before you know what happened. When you want to get out, you have to fight the undertow of other people's expectations. Through experience you learn to be a bit more self-controlled from the beginning.

Venus in Sagittarius

If wishes were horses, you and your lover would have a stable filled with the best thoroughbreds, and you would also have a few workhorses to get you through the tough times. You idealize relationships and want the philosophical heights along with the depths of feeling. You are great at planning romantic getaways and private interludes, designed to refresh your partnership.

You could be a great writer, as you have a powerful imagination, combined with a deep sensitivity. Your novels talk of romance in the midst of political instability and separations that only serve to strengthen the idealism of your characters. You enjoy traveling to places where you can envision your lovers meeting to renew their passion.

Venus in Capricorn

You value loyalty in your relationships, romantic or otherwise. You depend on your partner for consistency in all areas of the relationship. You may be a bit too "matter of fact" in your approach to romance for some partners. Because you feel the weight of responsibility in any partnership, you need to have a comparable level of trust in your lover.

You prefer seasoned partners. You don't want to have to teach anyone how to be a good mate. And you are willing to experiment with new things, as long as one of you knows what is involved.

You work best with people who have some experience. You can teach, but you prefer dedicated students who will do the work without having to be dragged along.

Venus in Aquarius

Your very progressive ideas about romantic relationships include more than one idea that goes beyond what is considered "normal." First and foremost, you want freedom within your relationship. However, the so-called open marriages of the late twentieth century may not be as attractive as they first appear. You have to find a balance between commitment and freedom if you are to be happy with your partner.

Your progressive ideas don't stop with sexuality. You bring innovation to your career, to organizations, and to any activity that keeps your attention long enough. Often you add an artistic touch to cooperative efforts, so that the finished package is far more elegant and satisfying.

Venus in Pisces

You long to find the love of your life, and you are willing to search for one lasting partnership. Sex is a big part of lasting satisfaction for you, but it isn't the only thing. Sex without love won't do. Because you are open to finding love, you may also be open to seduction before you know if there is a possibility for a lasting connection. Where relationships are concerned, you need to develop a sense of self-protection, even caution.

You have many musical and artistic interests, whether you are an artist or not. You appreciate the effort that goes into works of art, and you engage on the feeling level when you read, listen to music, or see artistic creations. Because mood is a powerful motivator, you cast your spell through scent, sight, sound, and touch, reaching deep within yourself and touching the depths in your partner.

The Second House

Venus is associated with two houses, the Second and the Seventh, which are the natural homes for Taurus and Libra. The Second House is the area of personal resources, and this is definitely not limited to money. Planets in the Second House indicate the form your resources take. They also indicate the people who influence you strongly in this area. They can show where your money comes from and where it goes. A strong material foundation provides you with the base from which to explore your other resources.

When there are no planets in this house, find the planet associated with the sign on the cusp of the Second House. That planet's position tells you which part of your life most directly impacts your personal resources.

- Physical resources include money and material goods. They encompass the objects that you own and your ability to work with material goods. They also include your talent and ability in moving around in the world.

- Mental resources include your education, ability to think logically, ability to make good decisions, and the ability to create plans. Your sense of order in your life is indicated by the sign(s) in the Second House.

- Emotional resources include your ability to engage deeply in feelings, to withdraw from a feeling in an appropriate manner, and to assist others in understanding and managing their feelings. Persistence is another quality associated with the Second House. When your emotions are involved, you often can stick to a task or an opinion very firmly.

- Spiritual resources include your sense of self and your position in the universe. This can include a concept of divinity or purpose. Often it is your spiritual resources that get you through the most difficult moments in life.

The Seventh House

The Seventh House reflects the quality of partnerships in your life. This includes romantic relationships, important community activities, and business partnerships. The Seventh House represents the "other," so in some ways anything outside yourself starts out as a Seventh-House thing, and moves into another department of your life as you come to know and understand it. For example, siblings are the "other baby" or "that baby" until they are understood as brothers and sisters.

Your encounters with other people throughout your life will color your sense of justice and balance. Their influence affects your willingness to engage in community activities, and sets the tone for your sense of obligation to the world outside yourself. The planets in the Seventh House indicate the kinds of people and experience that stimulate your awareness of your position in the world. They reflect the importance of partnership in your life. If there are no planets in this house, find the planet associated with the sign on the cusp of the Seventh House. The sign and house position of that planet tell you about another area of your life that strongly impacts partnerships.

The sign on the Seventh House indicates a very strong unconscious desire and idealism where partners are concerned. We are strongly attracted to romantic partners who have planets in that sign, particularly the Sun or Moon. Partners may have the Ascendant in that sign as well. The attraction is unconscious because we instinctively seek energies that balance our own, and the sign opposite your own Ascendant provides a comfortable balance or complement.

The Opposition Aspect

To be opposite, points in a chart are across the chart from each other, 180 degrees apart. Similar to what you read about the conjunction, the planets don't have to be exactly 180 degrees from each other, but they should be within 6 degrees of the exact opposition.

All of our ordinary senses work on the principle of polarity. To see, there must be light and dark. To hear, there must be presence and absence of sound waves, and we must be able to perceive the variation in amplitude. To feel, there is the object to be felt. The four personality types in Jungian psychology are composed of pairs. One type is conscious and the other in the pair is unconscious. If you are a Feeling type, then the Thinking function is less conscious; if you are Intuitive, then Sensation is necessarily your less conscious function.

When planets are opposite each other in the chart, they reflect the need for awareness. Think of yourself as the center of the chart. For energy to go from one planet to the other, it must pass directly through the center—through you. Thus we experience the opposition aspect directly, physically. If you are in the center of the chart, then one of the opposing planets is on one side of you, and the other is on the opposite side. You feel like you are standing between two people who are having a conversation. Because you are in the middle, you are very aware of what the two people (planets) are saying. We establish values through this kind of awareness. Is our experience pleasant or unpleasant? Positive or negative? Creative or destructive? This is one way we can establish our values and become aware of our own inner being.

To engage in the world, we need to be able to perceive it. We measure our position socially and materially through awareness. The opposition sometimes indicates areas where we project our unconscious ideas and feelings. We take the position of one planet and cast our feelings onto the other. As we develop awareness, we realize that our beliefs about people and things outside ourselves are sometimes projections that have found a convenient "hook" in the environment. As we reclaim the projection, we develop greater awareness.

Some astrologers characterize the opposition aspect as negative. Traditional astrology says the opposition connotes separation or pulling apart. Modern astrologers include this definition as part of a continuum of possibilities. If you are choosing between chocolate and vanilla ice cream, you don't have to feel pulled apart. Instead, feel the energy as the balance of a scale, weighing each choice. The same is true of any situation involving opposites.

Case Study: Celine Dion

Celine Dion has striking oppositions in her birthchart. She has Uranus and Pluto on one side, with Mercury and Venus on the other. Her chart even looks like a seesaw, with four planets in the lower half and the other six bundled closely together in the top half. Celine has a very public life as a singer, and she has a very private life with her husband and child.

Exercise

You have read about the Sun, Moon, Mercury, and now Venus. All of these planets are in the public sector of Celine's chart. Taking what you have read so far, look at her chart and consider what this means. You can read ahead about the other planets in her conjunctions and oppositions, or just use the keywords from the introduction.

1. Look at the signs for the Sun, Moon, Mercury, and Venus.
2. Look at the houses they are in (Eighth, Ninth, and Tenth).
3. Look at the conjunctions (Mercury-Venus, Sun-Saturn, and Moon-Mars). Look at the oppositions they form.

Even though you have not read the whole book, you were briefly introduced to the houses, signs, planets, and aspects in the introduction. Using the keywords found there, you should be able to construct a picture of how Celine tends to think and act.

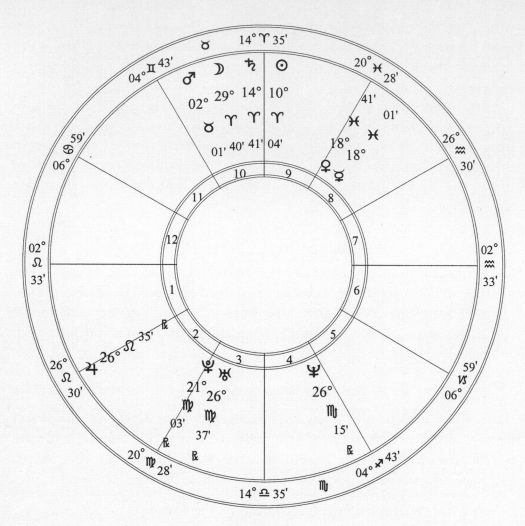

Chart 14
Celine Dion
March 30, 1968 / Charlemagne, Québec / 12:15 P.M. EST
Koch Houses

Case Study: Tiger Woods

Tiger also has strong oppositions in his chart. With seven planets and the Midheaven forming oppositions, we can expect him to be very aware of the world around him. Moon-Mars suggests that his energy depends on his emotional state. Mercury-Saturn indicates his attention to relationships with people much older or younger than himself. Jupiter-Pluto reflects the capacity to expand his will and power to gain awareness of conditions around him and other people in his life. Mars-Neptune shows his awareness of the balance of personal drive with compassion for others. Moon-Midheaven indicates that his deepest sources of personal strength are his family and his own emotional resources.

Exercise

Now look at your own chart.

1. Find the Sun, Moon, Mercury, Venus, and Ascendant.
2. Consider the signs and houses they occupy.
3. Notice if they are connected by aspects, especially conjunctions or oppositions.

Try to get a sense of how these different energies work together in your chart. Are they in compatible signs—same element or same mode? How do they relate to each other? Can you think of times when these energies were expressing really strongly in your life?

Summary

Venus in your astrological chart shows you something about the feminine principle. We have seen how harmony and beauty are powerful impulses to creativity, and we have considered the alter ego. We have also seen how the dynamics of awareness are grounded in apparent polarities. In the next chapter we add the concept of energy to our astrological formula. The planet Mars indicates how you actively engage in life. It shows how you use your personal qualities, as indicted by the Sun, Moon, Mercury, Venus, and Ascendant.

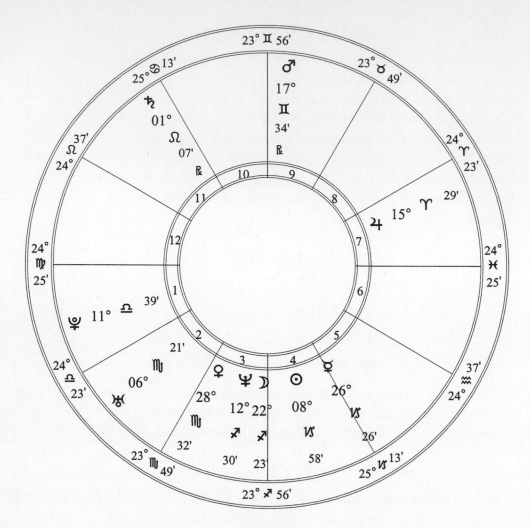

Chart 15

Tiger Woods

December 30, 1975 / Long Beach, CA / 10:50 P.M. PST

Koch Houses

8
Mars, the First House, and the Square

Mars is a planet of energy and action. In some respects that is all you need to know. Regardless of its placement in any chart, Mars shows where the action is. And that action is single-minded. It can be the ultimate indicator of self-centered activity. Mars is present when action turns to aggression. Because Mars is related to iron, it is also related to cutting instruments and to red blood cells. Mars energy that is out of control leads to accidents. As we pursue this line of thinking, we become aware of the less than positive side of this planet's energy.

There is a more creative side to Mars energy. We use energy for everything—muscle movement, power for machines of all kinds, and all creative actions. Mars plays a very positive role in our lives. The energy just needs some control. On a personal level the control comes from our minds. We are able to plan before we act, for example. We are able to consider the likely outcomes of our actions, and then we choose from among the actions we have available to us. It is only when we unconsciously spring-load our own egos and go off without thought that we get into serious trouble.

The two sides of Mars energy can be understood as the embodiment of action and desire. Action is the physical expression, and desire represents the more thoughtful side of this planet's energy. By considering these two very different expressions, you will get a well-rounded understanding of what Mars represents in the astrological chart.

Action

Even when we consider the active side of Mars, we find two distinctly different expressions of energy. Mars as the god of war is capable of sowing terror and panic in the enemy, as well as reflecting courage. These emotional responses are applicable in every area of our lives. If we think terror is something distant, we can think again. Do we not feel panic when we first go on stage? Is there some activity that inspires terror in you when you consider it? Do you have to muster your courage to go to the dentist, or even to get your hair cut? These emotions are a very real part of our daily lives.

The other side of Mars' active energy relates to something much more ordinary. As the god of agriculture, Mars was a god who encouraged the planting and tending of crops. While this takes a great deal of energy and attention on a daily basis, it is not the extreme action we associate with battles. The crops themselves use energy to break out of the seed, thrust roots down, and sprout upward. Mars is indicative of the action involved in every stage of life and growth.

Desire

Often we think of desire and action as being the same. They are actually two reflections of the energy of Mars. For one thing, desire is a mental process, while action is primarily physical. For another, desire takes many forms. There are physical desires for food, shelter, and clothing. Then there are sexual desires—for a partner with whom we can feel whole. There are mental desires—to write, to sculpt, or to have adventures through reading, movies, or the like. On a still higher plane, Mars reflects the desire for a spiritual teacher or path. Mars is at the core of religious expansion, as it reflects the desire to spread the word of God or Goddess.

Let's explore this desire business a bit more. Suppose you desire the taste and feel of Mexican food. You think through this desire and find that you have some choices. You can go to the store, purchase the necessary ingredients, and prepare the food. You can locate a Mexican restaurant and eat there. You can beg your friends to fulfill your desire for the food by cooking or taking you out to eat. You can sit with the desire, amplifying it until it becomes an obsession.

At some point you either forget about it or you take action. The desire side of Mars naturally moves into the action phase. You obtain food, one way or another, and it either is or is not Mexican food. Hunger will eventually drive the decision. A great deal of our planning time is spent in sorting through conflicting desires, determining the possible choices, and then acting on what we perceive to be the best choice available. Perhaps you have twenty dollars, but you know it has to buy food for several days. This makes the restaurant choice look less favorable. Ingredients for a Mexican dinner are inexpensive, for the most part. You discover that you already have some of them on your pantry shelf. You just need a few green chilis and some cheese. Now twenty dollars looks like it will go a lot further. The choice to make your own food involves a lot of action, so your Mars urge is partially satisfied in a second way.

The key to this somewhat problematic planet is to keep both desire and action in mind at the same time. We don't have to think very hard to project the likely outcomes of the actions we are considering. What is important is to think before we act. Most of the trouble associated with Mars is the result of acting first and thinking later.

Mars Through the Signs

Mars in Aries

Mars is very comfortable in Aries. Aries is the cardinal fire sign, and Mars is active and hot, which makes for a good match. This placement indicates a natural fighting spirit. There are strong urges that, with refinement and experience, become ambitions. You love independence and may fight to preserve it, even when you are ego-driven. Because of a headstrong tendency, there is the possibility of accidents, particularly to the head, an Aries part of the body.

Impatience is common with this placement of Mars. You have to work hard to contain your exuberant energy. Another way to deal with impatience is to direct it into some constructive activity. Physical exercise is a possibility. You can also pair Mars with another planet it aspects, to boost effectiveness in another area of your life. Directing your energy will produce better results than allowing the energy to rule you.

Mars in Taurus

Because Taurus is a sign of work and endurance, Mars here suggests strength and energy for the long haul. Aries may sprint; Taurus can run for miles, like a Masai warrior, maintaining a constant pace over long distances. Taurus is fixed earth, so there is a practical side to your energy. You are able to build your net worth, both financial and emotional, through consistent effort.

The downside is that you can become obstinate when you combine Mars' independence with Taurus' solidity. If you become totally invested in building your own little empire, you may lose sight of those things outside yourself that contribute to your success and happiness. The Masai warrior loves freedom, but is also part of a family and a culture. The very qualities of Mars in Taurus exemplified by the warrior are the ones that provide for continuity and stability.

Mars in Gemini

Gemini is a mutable air sign, thus Mars energy is less grounded and definitely less stable in this sign. There is tremendous mobility. The mental side of life is active and verbal ability is common. Of course your verbal expression can lean either to edgy criticism or enthusiastic encouragement—it's your choice. Throughout your life you may cultivate a variety of physical and mental skills, and then you integrate them into one powerful personal and vocational package.

All that Mars energy turned loose in a mutable air sign can lead to a scattered life with little sense of direction. You try on many different roles, and it takes time to settle on the one that is most comfortable for you. Often restless, you want to see more, do more, or at least do something new and different. Other factors in the birthchart usually balance these extreme tendencies. Thus you have periods of moving around, and then more grounded times. The hot air balloon lifestyle requires coming back down to refuel from time to time.

Mars in Cancer

This cardinal water sign offers a mixed welcome to Mars. On the one hand, Mars is very comfortable with cardinal energy, as both Mars and Cancer are active and directed, both strong Mars qualities. On the other hand, Mars may not be so comfortable in water. Basically a hot, dry sort of energy, Mars is not at its best here. The watery energy of Cancer may dampen the fires, or even seem to quench them altogether. On the third hand, fire and water make steam engines run. There is a powerful capacity to build up pressure and put it to good use.

You can experience benefits from your intense emotions, though at times you also experience the downside. For example, you enjoy novels and movies that feature intense action and even more intense feelings, and you see something of yourself reflected there. However, you may not enjoy being in the midst of such intensity in your own life. It is like feeling a rush of adrenaline: it is very invigorating, but you don't really want to live that way all the time. In addition, you usually are not fully conscious of your feelings. Once you learn to understand how your feelings work, however, you can put the fire/water energy to good use, creating energetic flow and direction in your life.

Mars in Leo

Leo is fixed fire. While Mars is not especially comfortable here, it does share the energy of fire. So on the face of things, Mars is well placed. However, the fixed nature of Leo is hard for independent Mars to endure. The compatible fire energy usually wins out, making Mars in Leo an indicator of self-confidence and composed activity. If Mars learns to look ahead, taking advantage of Leo's intuitive capacity, then most efforts lead to positive developments.

Mars in Leo sometimes reflects a self-centeredness that, when exaggerated, is very off-putting to others. The person with Mars here must cultivate an awareness of others in order to maintain enduring relationships. All the self-confidence in the world is not worth much when you are the only person willing to be around you. Thus the acquisition of wealth and power is most satisfying when you find ways to share with family, partners, and friends.

Mars in Virgo

Here is another sign where Mars is okay, but not great. Mars can thrive here, but it must find ways to be active that are rather contained and focused on details. The strength of Mars in Virgo is the capacity to exploit each situation. This depends on the ability to focus on the details, arrange them in some orderly pattern, and see into the pattern. Neatness has its appeal for Mars in Virgo. It may be important to consider all the details and not discard some of them too early in the game.

Mars here can become fussy and overly critical. You need to observe and understand the details, not criticize them. Another possible problem is that Mars' active energy may feel too restricted in this setting, causing nervous responses to rather minor difficulties.

Part of any good methodology for Mars in Virgo is to find opportunities to expend energy actively and often. Attention focused on work can be balanced with a workout or a walk to shift the focus.

Mars in Libra

Mars in Libra indicates enthusiasm for teamwork. In fact it indicates general enthusiasm. You are able to think through problems and devise cooperative solutions. You also are able to plan everything from coffee breaks to three-week vacations on other continents. You take the larger perspective and break it into workable units, and then you share the work with others in your family, social sphere, or work group.

You are subject to moods. Sometimes you cause major disagreements that won't even matter to you when the mood has passed, yet you will have to deal with the consequences. Usually quick on the trigger, you may need to cultivate patience. If you wait even five minutes, often you will find you have changed your own mind. In this way you preserve those oh-so-important relationships.

Mars in Scorpio

For you the survival instinct is powerful. This is a good thing, but it can also be a bad thing. Sometimes the instinct activates responses that are way out of proportion to the problem. Then you find yourself in full armor with sword ready, when one calm sentence would have been adequate. On the positive side, you are able to get through literal and metaphorical life-threatening situations, emerging none the worse for wear. In fact you amaze people with your resilience.

You desire control and power. It's that simple. You seek the job or position with the most clout, or you do the most meaningful work you can find. Within your search for power, you carefully formulate and pursue your personal goals as well. While it is possible for you to exert your power to fit in with others, eventually you plan to rise to the top, and if deterred from this goal, you often gain a better position by moving on to another company, and even a new career.

Mars in Sagittarius

You have an innate philosophical orientation, and you study things before you speak out. When you finally say your piece, you want to be heard and believed by others. Thus you are careful to document your views with facts and figures. Much of the information you gather goes into a data pool from which you can extract the pertinent facts, fit them together into a working hypothesis, and test their validity.

At heart you are an adventurer. You love to travel, and may choose a career that frequently takes you away from your home base. Whether at home or away, you enjoy a variety of sports, and like to participate as well as watch. Extreme sports are not daunting, except where age is a factor, and even then you are willing to try things just so you can say you did.

Mars in Capricorn

Mars in Capricorn has plenty of energy to put into any concrete project. You are certain that you can complete any task you undertake, and do it well. You rarely fail because you continue to put effort into accomplishing your goals, perhaps long after others would have given up.

Because you have such a high success rate, you also have a high opinion of yourself. Eventually the time arrives when you overestimate your capabilities. Previously you experienced glorious successes, but now you crash and burn in defeat. Your enemies should never count you out, though, as you can rise again from the lowest position to the heights of power.

You are strongly independent, so when your acquaintances have abandoned you for dead, you don't mind having time to redesign your life. You know there will be plenty of time to reveal yourself when you have made your comeback. You are nothing if not ambitious.

Mars in Aquarius

You are obsessed with freedom. It is so important to you that you would rather leave a secure position than experience restrictions of any kind. Even when you must follow someone else's lead, your mind is off in your own personal wonderland of thoughts and feelings. Freedom can become the foundation of an argumentative nature, as you take an opposing position just for the sake of being different.

Another way to manage when you can't have absolute freedom is to be the one in charge. You love to go into a problem situation and find ways to resolve all the difficulties and differences of opinion. You love to get those folks organized or possibly reorganized to suit your own taste. Your talent for logic provides the ability to convince others that your way of thinking is the only right way. The upside is that you do the necessary thinking beforehand, and at each step along the way.

Mars in Pisces

You relish the concept of being in a private, even secret, group. First, you like secrets. You enjoy the feeling of knowing more than the other person. Second, you are not one to seek the limelight. You prefer to work in seclusion, and you choose topics suited to the venue. You find the so-called occult sciences attractive, and may even perform ceremonial magic or spells.

Then you find you have to struggle for recognition. You do so much of your work in private that others don't associate the results with you as much as with your publicist or social secretary. You need to balance your secretive nature with social skills that bring you into the public eye.

Mars in Pisces is susceptible to drug and alcohol abuse. You should avoid tobacco as well. Moderation may seem like a nice concept, but you find you are not always able to maintain it. To be known, you must be both more visible and more reliable.

The Mars Cycle—Evaluating Action

The monthly cycle of the Moon is a familiar event in our lives. The annual cycle of the Sun is another, providing for birth, growth, and maturation of all living things. The Mars cycle is somewhat longer than that of the Sun and is quite personal in its expression. Alexander Ruperti, a German osteopath and astrologer, studied the cycles of the planets in relation to his patients' physical complaints. He described the interrelationship between the cycles of the Sun and Mars in great detail. He said that when Mars is closest to the Earth—and therefore opposing the Sun in your chart—any problem you have with Mars will have to be resolved.[1]

Astrology provides more than one way to look at the Mars cycle. I prefer to look at Mars as it reaches the square, opposition, or conjunction to its own place in the birthchart, as this shows when Mars' own energy is being activated most strongly. The squares challenge us to take effective action, the oppositions provide awareness, and the conjunction begins a new cycle of activity approximately every two years. You can read about the square aspect later in this chapter.

The First House

The First House is the part of the chart that begins with the Ascendant, or rising sign. This house was the first part of the birthchart to rise in the east after the time of birth. Let's be clear from the very beginning that the First House is different from the Ascendant. The Ascendant is the point in space that was on the eastern horizon at the time of birth. It is a personal point in the chart that can be used to describe your persona, or what you show to the world. At the same time the persona you show to the world can affect how you see and experience the world. For example, a daredevil approach to the world tends to attract daredevil results.

The First House is the section of the birthchart that indicates what is important to each of us as individuals. It includes a portion of the sign on the Ascendant and generally includes part or all of the next sign, depending on the latitude and time of birth. The First House reflects the physical body, so in that sense it is similar to the Ascendant. However, it covers far more than just the physical body and personality.

The reason for this broader meaning is that we have to consider the planets associated with the First House, and also any planets in the First House. This colors the nature of this part of one's life significantly. Also, the houses represent areas of our lives. The First House reflects personal activities and the personal space we call our own. It is the environment of infancy and early childhood. Planets in the First House indicate how we engage in the environment around us—what our tastes are, how we relate physically to the world, and those things we consider to be private.

Case Study: Henri Toulouse-Lautrec

Here is an example of the difference between the Ascendant and the First House. Henri Toulouse-Lautrec had Scorpio on the Ascendant. He also had Sun, Jupiter, and Mercury in the First House. His chart was used as an example in the Ascendant chapter (chapter 5), so you have already seen what his persona was like. Now we will consider his physical appearance, his health, and something about how he moved around in his environment.

Lautrec's Sun was in Sagittarius. You already have an idea of what this means. To review, Sagittarius is an intuitive sign. Lautrec had the potential for a deeply philosophical view of life. He had the potential to be a fine sportsman, interested in riding particularly. He was an optimistic sort, especially as a child. His life reflects a certain restlessness.

Physically Sagittarius is associated with the hips and thighs. Lautrec had the great misfortune to have a bone disease, most likely a genetic disorder (his parents were first cousins, and he was not the only family member with the bone disorder). During his childhood he broke one leg and then the other, necessitating very long recuperative periods. In reading accounts, one has to wonder about the medical care he received. In the end he was very short, with legs disproportionately short for the size of his body. He had to be very careful not to reinjure himself, and he was unable to participate in the sports that his father so loved. This was a great disappointment to everyone in the family. In spite of all that, Lautrec traveled, lived on his own, and managed to establish himself as an artist.

Jupiter and Mercury are also in Sagittarius. You will read about Jupiter later in the book in chapter 9, and you have already read about Mercury. Lautrec was forthright in speech and studied extensively. He began his religious training in early childhood. As we have already seen, he did scatter his energies, indulging in women, parties, and alcohol. At the same time he produced a significant body of artistic work.

You met Jupiter briefly in the first part of the book, so you know this planet is expansive. With Jupiter in the First House we might expect a weight problem. Lautrec was a very short man with an upper body sized for much longer legs. Although he was not fat, he appeared bulky because of his short stature. His expansiveness included his wide group of friends, many of whom his parents disliked. He also painted large, brilliant images. He did little to avoid excess in drink.

Lautrec wrote letters, and in several languages. In this we can see his expansive (Jupiter) communication (Mercury) skills. He wrote passionately about himself and what he was doing and also about his feelings (Sun). It is through his writing that we can come to know more about him as an individual, and see what he chose to show to the world.

The Square Aspect

You may recall from the introduction that the square aspect is 90 degrees and that it represents challenges in the astrological chart. Traditional astrologers were not as kind as I was when I chose the word *challenge*. The square was formerly grouped with the opposition and sometimes the conjunction, and they were called "hard" aspects. This meant

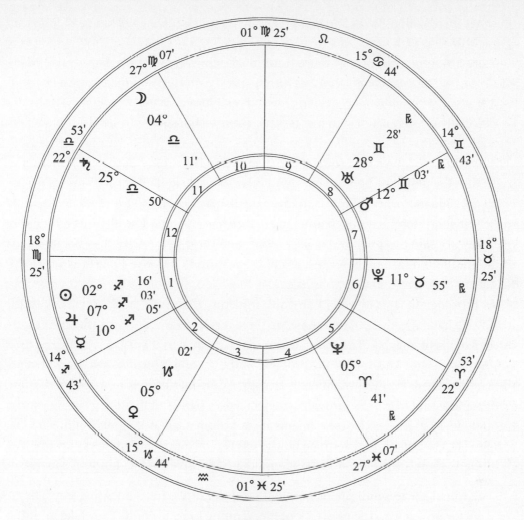

Chart 16
Henri Toulouse-Lautrec
November 24, 1864 / Albi, France / 6:00 A.M. LMT
Koch Houses

that they were both difficult and solid. The square represented a wall to be climbed, an obstacle in your path to be overcome.

Here are some examples of more traditional delineations of the Sun square Mars: *You limit yourself emotionally. You lack direction and planning, and thus waste a lot of energy. Every square in a natal chart is a cross to bear. Squares represent conflict.* This is not an especially positive set of statements. Let's examine the square to see what it actually means.

The geometric form of a square, or 90 degree angle, is used in the construction of buildings; the design of books, boxes, and other objects; and all sorts of things we use every day. Square corners allow us to make regular shapes and to avoid waste. Recently some fast-food stores have begun making square hamburgers. The obvious reasons are that they are easier to prepare, package, cook, and serve. Otherwise they would be the traditional round shape. These are a few of the reasons to perceive squares as very helpful aids in daily living, and not obstacles at all.

In astrology squares represent obvious, sometimes "in your face" contacts with the world. We have already seen that there are three modes in which energy functions: cardinal, fixed, and mutable. The cardinal signs are separated by 90 degrees, as are the fixed and mutable signs. This reveals the problem of the square: it involves two signs that are the same mode of energy, but different elements. Consider planets in Aries and Cancer. Both planets want to express through cardinal (active) signs, but they are trying to express through fire and water, and these elements are not compatible. Water puts out fire. It's that simple. The challenge is to determine how to use two incompatible energies effectively.

Because there are three modes of energy, there are three distinct kinds of squares:

- **Cardinal squares** indicate planets that want to express in an outgoing way. They vie for position on the racetrack of life, wanting to be in front. They take us out into the world, where we may experience little or no protection. With cardinal squares, we feel rather insecure.

- **Fixed squares** are very different. They take us into ourselves, revealing two energies that vie for position in determining what our inner processes will be. This is more like two ideas, beliefs, or feelings chasing each other around the bush, trying to establish supremacy, and not going anywhere at all.

- **Mutable squares** show where internal energy is linked to the outward-moving energy of mind. There is potential for harmony with mutable squares because they use both the outgoing energy associated with cardinal signs and the internal processes associated with fixed signs. However, this flexible energy is hard to pin down. It is constantly changing, adapting, and resolving whatever inconsistencies it finds. This square reflects a situation where you can't seem to make a firm decision involving the two planetary energies.

All three types of squares connect us to the material world because they reflect action in the physical realm. They are obvious to us and to the people around us. Whether we are outgoing and direct, internally occupied, or indecisive, other people can see the results of the square's activity in our lives.

Clearly there is a downside to the square aspect, but there is also a definite upside. Squares represent conditions that press us into action. We must face them and deal with them, even when we wish they would just go away. By facing them, we develop strengths like courage, determination, and perseverance. We learn that we can live through difficulties because we have learned to blend or bend energies for our own use in the past. As we learn to accept challenges more openly, we find that we turn challenges into advantages. We develop practical skills to deal with everyday problems. We also learn to respond intelligently to problems instead of reacting without thought.

Another thing we learn is that when a square aspect demands a response, we cannot ignore the energies of the square easily. We learn to assess the situation of the square, determine what is involved as well as we can, and then make a decision about what action to take. We learn how to reduce the friction of the situation, how to moderate our feelings, and how to test the situation to obtain additional information. In the process we learn how to handle similar situations in the future. These last two sentences embody the nature of all three kinds of squares: the outgoing, the inward focusing, and the mediating.

Case Study: Mike Bloomberg

Mike Bloomberg has had an outrageously successful business career. He amassed a personal fortune of billions of dollars and had an information-based company that provided data for the stock market and revolutionized the way market business is transacted. In his chart the closest aspect is Moon square Mars.

Then he decided he wanted to be the mayor of New York City. He gathered people together to help him, he put down a lot of his own money (some reports go as high as 40 million dollars), and he set out to become mayor. He said that when he asked people what they thought of the idea, they told him, "Don't do it." This sounds a lot like Moon square Mars. They pointed out all the usual reasons: the emotional strain, the potential damage to his reputation, the physical strain, the time away from his own business, etc. Mike decided to go for it anyway. That also sounds like Moon square Mars. He likes a challenge, and he has almost endless energy to put into a task when he is interested.

Then the World Trade Center was attacked and destroyed. Mike is running for mayor of a city that had enormous problems before September 11, 2001. Now he is on line to deal with a single event that caused untold physical, political, emotional, and even spiritual damage. Moon square Mars, in fixed signs, makes me wonder if he may have had at least one conversation with himself in which he said, "What have I gotten myself into this time? I sure didn't see this coming. What do I do now?"

In a letter to his fellow New Yorkers in February 2003, published on the Internet, Mike Bloomberg itemized the 380 campaign promises he made, and listed the progress made toward fulfilling each of them. He stated that 80 percent had been fulfilled or were in process, 5 percent turned out to be inappropriate directions for the city, and 15 percent were incomplete because of budget constraints. He also stated that he welcomes scrutiny of city government because accountability leads to better performance in both the private and public sectors.[2]

Because this square has been there his whole life, Mike has had to face it before. We know because of his huge business success that he has learned to think through problems carefully, weigh the options, and make good decisions. Now, when his strengths are on the line, he has shown that he can analyze the situation from a lot of angles, consider the demands for short-term and long-term problem solving, and mobilize a team of people to get the job under way. We see that the Moon-Mars square can reflect big challenges, and that it also reflects the potential for strength and determination.

Exercise

Find Mars in your birthchart.

1. Think about the sign your natal Mars is in and how that reflects your energy.

2. Look at your Mars aspects. Make a list of them, and write down a description for each of them.

3. Think about how you do—or don't—perceive those kinds of action in your life.

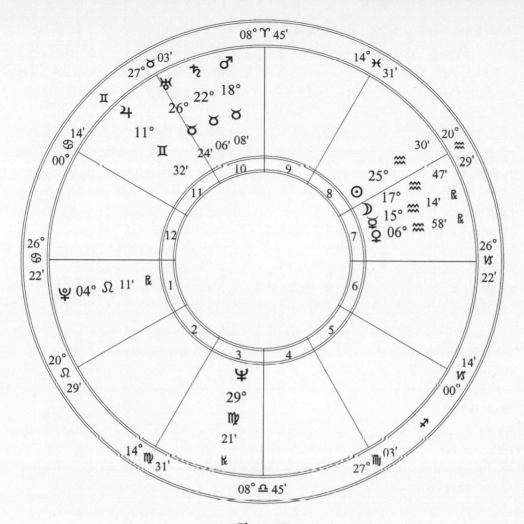

Chart 17
Mike Bloomberg
February 14, 1942 / Brighton, MA / 3:40 P.M. EST
Koch Houses

Summary

Mars represents the energy we use every day in all our activities. Sometimes sexual, sometimes angry, Mars energy can also be steady, persuasive, and even devoted. Mars is associated with the First House and Aries in the chart, and shares some of the "Me-me-me" qualities found there.

Energy drives all our actions, and Mars is the planet that indicates energy in the horoscope. When well placed by sign and well aspected, Mars shows an active, prosperous life. Some Mars placements can indicate problems, and this is where you engage intellect, intuition, and will to overcome life's challenges. In the next chapter on the planet Jupiter, we will see how all that energy is balanced by our philosophical perspective. We also will see how processes work in our lives.

---

1. Alexander Ruperti, *Cycles of Becoming* (Davis, Calif.: CRCS Publications, 1978) 99.

2. http://home.nyc.gov/html/om/pdf/campaign_accountability_report.pdf

9
Jupiter, the Ninth House, and the Sextile

Jupiter is by far the largest of the planets in our solar system. Its moon Ganymede is larger than the planet Mercury, and Callisto is not far behind. Its numerous moons make this planet a spectacular sight, whether through a telescope or through the lens of Voyager cameras.

Jupiter is the planet that reflects function and process in your birthchart. For most practical purposes, the form of things we perceive is rigid and relatively changeless. Atoms form molecules, and the molecules group together in certain predictable ways. Similarly, the planets reflect certain kinds of energy, and that energy is fairly predictable. Where Jupiter is involved in an aspect, we can investigate the function of each energy, and through this study we can adapt the function of each planet's energy to fit our own needs.

Jupiter expands our thinking. We are used to living within the range of our own experience, and we each have our personal experience of planetary energies. When Jupiter aspects a planet, there is a condition in which we can expand our thinking about that planet. For example, we have looked at Mercury in terms of communication. Mercury is in a particular sign and house, indicating the tone of communication in general and the area of life where it takes on greater significance. An aspect from Jupiter reflects a greatly expanded significance, and Jupiter's sign and house show the nature of that expansive quality.

Function or Process

Jupiter reflects function on every level of life. It relates to developmental processes from early childhood to the end of life. Without growth and change we would find life very dull. Jupiter adds faith, vision, and understanding to all our activities.

Physical

Assimilation, digestion, liver, blood, organ function. From the beginning of life Jupiter is active. Cells grow and divide to form an embryo, which develops into a fetus. When expansion and growth have reached optimum conditions, the infant is born. At this point the newly independent life has to continue to grow if it is to thrive. Jupiter is related to vitamin B_6, which makes the absorption of other vitamins possible. Digestion would be ineffective without this essential nutrient. Jupiter also governs biotin and choline, two essentials for the proper metabolism of fats and proteins.

Jupiter is associated with the liver, the blood, and the function of organs in general. Thus the function of cleansing the body and carrying nutrients to the cells is reflected by Jupiter in the birthchart. We are coming to understand the importance of a proper diet in the maintenance of optimum health, and we can see that Jupiter is a key player.

Mental

Learning and philosophy. Throughout our lives we are constantly expanding our mental capabilities. From the moment of birth we take in information and process it at an incredible rate. Jupiter reflects the primary direction for learning and philosophical outlook.

Emotional

Expanded experience. Emotional expansion comes through the desire to engage with other people and to have more and deeper experiences. In the process we learn how to gain such experiences without causing harm to others. We learn to seek harmony amid the other qualities of experience.

Spiritual

Aspiration toward the divine. Beyond physical, mental, and emotional desires, most of us feel the need for spiritual fulfillment. Jupiter reflects expansion in this direction as well. Jupiter's sign, house placement, and aspects form a picture of how you develop as a spiritual being.

Jupiter Through the Signs

Jupiter in Aries

Jupiter's desire to expand is reflected in Aries through a lack of balance. There is an impulse to expand that carries you forward into more and more activities. You may find that you achieve results before you are actually ready to act on the outcomes, and this places you in a vulnerable position.

You enjoy being in expensive, elegant surroundings. This is all right as long as you don't make those purchases in anticipation of money that could be delayed, or worse, never arrive. Honesty is part of your makeup, so you don't want to do anything that would damage your credibility.

Jupiter in Taurus

You are generous toward others, and you are usually generous with yourself. You want to build financial security for yourself, but your spending habits can get in the way of practical savings and investment for the future.

Excesses of any kind can lead to illness. Thus attention to diet is indicated, as well as moderation in all activities. You are open to many ideas, and you enjoy your creature comforts.

You may become a trustee for another person, or the executor of the estate of a deceased person. You have the financial skills to manage either position well.

Jupiter in Gemini

You go where the wind takes you, and you go willingly. You love to run around the neighborhood, and your concept of neighbors may extend to other continents. You are genuinely nice, and your diplomatic nature allows you to fit into the crowd wherever you find yourself.

You not only love a change of scene, you love changes of all kinds. The multiple connections you form over the course of your childhood, studies, and career make you the consummate networker. If people experience only six degrees of separation from others, it is because of people like you who draw up the map of connections and find the shortest distance between two people.

Jupiter in Cancer

Your feelings expand to encompass not only your nuclear family, but your extended family and your social sphere as well. You are receptive to input from all of these people, and you form a hub of exchange for feelings and information among this wider group of individuals.

You must remember that you are open to the psychic energies of others. This means that you have a way of interpreting the jungle drums even when they are very quiet. Don't jump to conclusions about what is going on around you, as you may be wrong. It is important to examine your intuitions, and then ask questions that are designed to confirm or disprove your conclusions. Then you are positioned to help maintain or restore the equilibrium of the family system.

Jupiter in Leo

Self-confidence is your calling card. You are able to take on huge projects, lay the groundwork, do the necessary planning, and then bring together a team of individuals to make the whole thing happen right on cue. Your leadership skills improve with every venture, as does your popularity. This is because you give generous credit wherever it is due.

You are a staunch member of your own fan club. Your egotism can get in the way of success if you don't temper it, or at least disguise it in some way. What is needed is some introspective activity like meditation, or even the practice of a martial art. In this way you develop awareness of your own inner life, and you become less self-absorbed.

Jupiter in Virgo

You love detail, that's all there is to it. You examine your values, your thoughts, your feelings in detail, and as a result you have an orderly mind and an orderly lifestyle. Because of your orderly approach, you are able to get a lot more work done than most people.

You take a few minutes to organize your work, and you thereby save hours of time duplicating your efforts and searching for lost items.

You are a harmonious team member. You work well with others, and you are capable of leading when it is your turn. You see the value of interaction among team members, and you also understand the importance of having a chain of command. You are ambitious, and others may see you as dangerous in this regard. At other times you take a devil-may-care attitude, seeming to care not at all about the group effort.

Jupiter in Libra

You would make a good judge, as you have a sense of justice. When you understand the rules clearly, you are the ideal person to referee the game, as you exemplify fairness. Public office suits your qualities very well, as long as you keep your eye on the goal and don't get distracted with side offers.

You tend to rely on other people to do what they say they will, much as you do what you promise. You are disappointed when others fail to place the same degree of importance on their responsibilities. One way to keep others moving in the desired direction is to check in with them frequently, even when there is no problem. They develop a sense of closeness and support that way.

Jupiter in Scorpio

Your materialism can get out of hand if you are not careful. You love new sensations of all kinds and can overindulge in foods, sexual relationships, and other pleasures. Cravings can lead to a ruthless quest for greater excitement. You sometimes overrate your potential.

You also have a generally optimistic view of life. You believe your needs and desires will be met, and they usually are. You can look to Saturn's placement for help in controlling your expansive desires, and you can look to Mercury for hints on how to develop more logical thinking about your goals.

Jupiter in Sagittarius

You are a pillar of justice. You would campaign for cats if you saw one being mistreated, or elm trees if you felt they needed attention. You spend just as much time focused on your inner life, seeking to develop and maintain a strong moral and ethical perspective.

Your capacity for planning can carry you into new markets in your business, to new countries in your travels, and to new subjects of study. You can balance several lines of thought and keep them moving forward, so you manage to get schoolwork done in the midst of extracurricular activities. Ultimately you develop a strong sense of personal values, rooted in religious or philosophical precepts that you may have learned as a child, and developed through your studies.

Jupiter in Capricorn

Your sense of responsibility is strong where it is needed, and it may be intrusive where it is not required. You are not in charge of the world, and you don't have to take responsibility for everything that happens. Still, your strong leadership is built on your ability to take the heat for your team members. You have the talent of keeping one eye on the goal and the other on weaker team members, helping them do their very best.

Don't get a big head just because you are nearly always successful. Remember, you couldn't do it without the rest of the team. Your family and associates deserve a lot of credit for their contributions.

Because your ideas are an open book, people may count on something you mention, and be hurt when you do something different. You benefit from learning how to clearly state your opinions and distinguish them from decisions. You establish your trustworthy character in this way.

Jupiter in Aquarius

Your ideas are all over the map. Hopes and wishes expand to take up the available space, and there is plenty of brainpower there to fuel your schemes and dreams. You revel in planning, taking joy in the prospect of all things new. The challenge is to prioritize clearly and logically.

You have a deep understanding of human nature. You can generally get to the bottom of anyone's concerns by listening to them and then restating the problem clearly. You enjoy being around other people and have become a trained observer of human behavior. Your "street smarts" are better than years of book learning in this regard.

Jupiter in Pisces

Supersensitive, you can tell what each guest is feeling within five minutes of the time they walk in the door. Sometimes, however, the mixture of feelings can be overwhelming. This is especially true if you are indulging in alcohol or if there are a lot of smokers around you. Thus, while you enjoy a good party, you need to be sensible in what you consume.

Your exemplary kindness can be your greatest asset. It can also be misplaced on people who seek to take advantage of your open heart. To maintain balance between your inner life and a life of caring for others, you need time alone to meditate, to pursue your own interests, or simply to vegetate. What seems like a waste of time to others is your spiritual refueling time.

Jupiter Through the Houses

Expansion, function, process. Physical, mental, emotional, spiritual. These are the keys to Jupiter's action in each house of your chart. Each house in your chart is associated with a specific part of the body. Jupiter's house placement highlights one physical function or area of the body for you. The idea is that you tend to be aware of the function of one part of the body more than others, and that area or function serves as a metaphor for mental, emotional, and spiritual concerns.

Jupiter in the First House

The entire body and its function is of interest, with a particular focus on the head. The relationship of the head to the body depends on vision and hearing. Metaphorical vision is central to your mental and physical activity.

Jupiter in the Second House

The neck and throat are a focal point. Your physical voice provides the means to communicate with the world, and is also the carrier of your spiritual voice. Hearing and balance are your most critical functions.

Jupiter in the Third House

The breathing process is central to all your activities, and the condition of the breath affects your mental and emotional well-being. Thyroid function is another focal point.

Jupiter in the Fourth House

Digestion and assimilation are key processes. Jupiter's presence here may indicate sensitivity to certain foods. You are also sensitive to mental, emotional, and spiritual intake of all kinds.

Jupiter in the Fifth House

You alternate between physical indulgence and mental activities. You have creative talent in both the physical and mental arenas. You are self-aware and self-confident.

Jupiter in the Sixth House

You are able to resist disease through both physical and mental means. You may put forth significant effort to understand how you assimilate nutrients, and you may want to examine your personal learning style as well.

Jupiter in the Seventh House

Kidney function is a focal point for you. The kidneys purify the blood and remove toxins from the body. You may need to develop ways to detoxify emotionally as well, and meditation can help.

Jupiter in the Eighth House

The muscular systems and sexual organs are areas where you focus your attention. Healthy processes of both depend on mental as well as physical conditioning.

Jupiter in the Ninth House

Your physical power comes from the hip and thigh region of the body. With the proper mental attitude, you have great strength and endurance.

Jupiter in the Tenth House

Your joints in general, and the knees in particular, are the focus of your physical concerns. Flexibility is the main concern for you, and this includes physical, mental, social, and spiritual flexibility.

Jupiter in the Eleventh House

Circulation and the oxygenation of the blood are functions you focus on throughout your life. Ideas energize you mentally and emotionally in the same way oxygen powers your body.

Jupiter in the Twelfth House

You give a good deal of attention to your feet and how they function. If they are comfortable, you are able to explore the world easily. You seek to broaden your emotional and spiritual understanding as well.

The Jupiter Cycle

Jupiter takes about twelve years to go around the Sun. This cycle provides a signpost for all kinds of development. Before the modern era, very few people lived to see age sixty. In fact, the average life expectancy was closer to thirty-six. Thus children were expected to mature and enter the world of productive adulthood much more quickly. The contemporary life span is more in the range of sixty-five years plus, and therefore adult developmental processes are more significant to us than at any previous time in history.

In many cultures, people acknowledge the passage of the first twelve-year cycle of Jupiter with rituals. World religions have coming-of-age ceremonies at about age twelve, and most students are at the transition point from grade school to middle or junior high school at this time. However, children are generally not legally responsible until later. Most states provides special driver's licenses for sixteen-year-olds, and most children are not tried as adults for crimes until age eighteen, the halfway point in the second Jupiter cycle. The U.S. Constitution was amended in 1971 to allow eighteen-year-olds to vote in all elections, and the states ratified this amendment quickly. One reason for this was purely pragmatic—if they hadn't done so, they would have had to run state and local elections separate from federal elections.

Coming of Age

The following brief descriptions of the Jupiter cycles include approximate ages when they begin, and some significant childhood and adult developmental stages associated with them.

Coming of Age Physically

At age twelve, many world religions and cultures have a coming-of-age ceremony to welcome children into the ranks of adulthood. These ceremonies acknowledge that young people are ready to enter society as young adults. New roles often include sexuality (or at least puberty), responsibility, and spirituality.

Coming of Age Intellectually

By age twenty-four, we have completed regular schooling and are either out in the world working or continuing our education in college. More people pursue higher education now to enhance earning ability and to broaden their interests and understanding of the world in other areas.

Coming of Age Emotionally

By age thirty-six, we have experienced the world on our own and have learned a great deal about our social responsibilities. By this time we may have changed our beliefs about what we are seeking emotionally. We feel the weight of adult responsibilities by this time, and we seek more fulfilling emotional experiences.

Coming of Age Spiritually

Around age thirty-six, and certainly at around age forty-eight, we have come full circle with the ordinary functioning of our lives. We find, sometimes, that we are still seeking to know more and to find greater understanding. Many people are looking for a second vocation that is more satisfying.

After Middle Age

Even later in life we continue to aspire to a deeper understanding of the nature of our lives and the nature of spirit. Jupiter shows the primary direction of spiritual aspiration, and it also indicates, by its relationships to other planets, how our lives develop all along the way. Age sixty is close to the common retirement age. Yet we see people retiring early from one vocation to pursue something quite different, and we also see people continuing to work for many years after age sixty because they are capable to continuing and interested in remaining active.

As we continue through the later chapters, we will see that Saturn and the outer planes have dynamic cycles as well. Some of these cycles culminate at the same time, indicating a doubling of influences. For example, two and one-half Jupiter cycles is roughly the same as one Saturn cycle. Thus the midcycle awareness we noticed at age eighteen is repeated around the time of endings and new beginnings associated with the Saturn Return, which occurs between the ages of twenty-eight and thirty.

In the next chapter we will look at Saturn, the planet that reflects structure in our lives. You will see that there are two times when the cycles of Jupiter and Saturn come together: first around age twenty-eight to thirty, and again at age fifty-six to sixty. These are times when we must come to terms with how structural boundaries interface with our desire for expanded activity. At around age thirty, we gain awareness of the relationship of function and structure. At around age sixty, we take a more philosophical view— we are more skillful in how we get things done.

The Ninth House

The Ninth House is associated with higher thought. Education beyond the legal requirements falls in this category. There is also a connection to travel, another Ninth-House matter, because we often leave home to attend a college or university. It is at this level that we develop personal mastery of one or more studies, and we begin to see our own beliefs as separate from those of family and society.

In addition, higher thought includes religion, philosophy, and contemplative practice. We are often taught a religion and its practices as children. Even if this does not happen, as we mature we are exposed to the beliefs of other people, and we compare them to our own. Many people find new and different religious interests as adults. We develop the capacity for contemplation over the years, and we often find that we become more flexible in our beliefs.

A third concern is the law. By law we mean moral and ethical codes in general, not just the legal system. Whether associated with religious beliefs or not, we depend on a system of laws to guide our daily activities. We more or less agree on what is "proper" or "right," and we have courts to help resolve issues when our rights are violated. The Ninth House may indicate legal matters that arise during your life.

Another Ninth House matter is long-distance travel, which generally includes travel to foreign countries and across oceans. I have found that we each have a definition of "long distance." For some people going "up state" is a long trip, while others define travel to another hemisphere or even into space as long distance.

Finally, the Ninth House includes our individual spiritual leanings, apart from formal religion and organized philosophy. This is the house that reflects personal values— values that transcend family, society, and culture. Some of what we are taught sticks to us throughout life, and some lessons are dropped in favor of different beliefs. The Ninth

House indicates how this occurs and when, and also indicates the direction in which we seek deeper spiritual experience.

The Sextile Aspect

The sextile aspect (60 degrees) is not related to sex per se. Rather, it reflects the opportunities that enter our lives, either as the potential reflected in the birthchart or as planets move forward to form aspects. Yes, some of these opportunities will be of a sexual nature, and the metaphor is a good one. An opportunity is a situation where two or more factors come together and suggest additional possibilities. These opportunities can be in any area of experience.

Generally the planets in a sextile aspect are in compatible elements—either fire and air, or earth and water. The two planets animate each other, reflecting an awareness of situations in our lives that show promise. If we perceive the value of the associations, and if we grasp the opportunity, then change occurs, based on our effectiveness in using what we know to help that change along.

The sextile aspect involves three things. First, there is the opportunity itself. The planets in the aspect, the signs, and the houses they occupy describe the nature of the opportunity. Second, we have to be aware of the opportunity. We have to be looking for something new and different. Third, we have to make a decision and take action for the opportunity to manifest. They say that "opportunity knocks," and we have to open the door. Without an active response, the opportunity will not develop.

Case Study: Madonna

Madonna, now in her forties, is a mother, a movie star, and an outrageously successful performer. She has been able to place herself in the right place at the right time with the right stuff ever since the ninth grade. At age seventeen, she left Michigan for New York, after graduating a semester early from high school. In 1979 she did nude photos for *Playboy* and *Penthouse*, and she has continued to use her sexual presence to earn massive amounts of money.

Madonna's birthchart has a close grouping of planets in the Twelfth House sextiling another group in the Second House. In addition, Venus, the planet of beauty and art, sextiles the Midheaven in Gemini. She has had multiple opportunities for a successful career. I want to discuss just one of the many sextiles: the Sun in Leo sextile Jupiter in

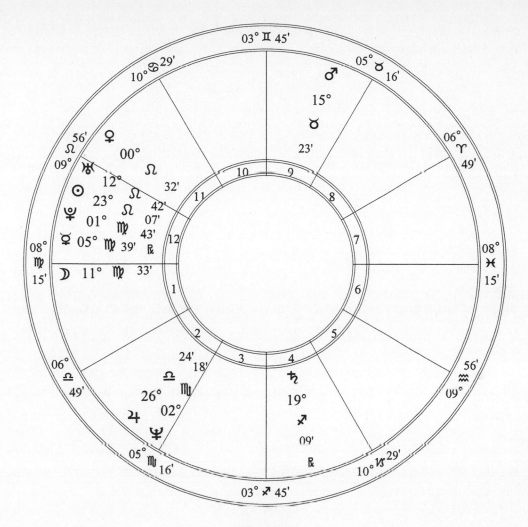

Chart 18

Madonna

August 16, 1958 / Bay City, MI / 7:05 A.M. EST

Koch Houses

Libra. This aspect promises health, recognition, and advancement in life. There is success in both the material and the spiritual spheres, if the opportunities of this aspect are grasped.

The downside of the Sun-Jupiter sextile is a materialistic attitude. "Material Girl" certainly speaks to this side of Madonna's career goals. The desire and will to expand and achieve success is not a bad thing in itself. The less constructive outcomes often involve extravagant spending and unattractive displays of wealth. Privacy—and secrecy— are associated with the Twelfth House. Because of her great success and public notoriety, Madonna values her privacy a great deal. But with four planets in the Twelfth House, privacy is difficult for her to maintain.

The Sun-Jupiter sextile reflects the course of Madonna's career path. When Jupiter came back to its birth degree in 1970, Madonna was already expressing herself via whatever means were available. While she apparently performed well academically in high school, she has a reputation for having performed sexually as well. By July of 1970, Madonna knew what she wanted out of life, and fame was definitely a part of that equation. At that time Mars was in the sign of Cancer, forming a square to Jupiter, thereby adding a lot of energy to the equation.

At her second return of Jupiter to its birth degree, Madonna was well on her way to fame and fortune. November of 1981 was a very significant time for her astrologically. In addition to Jupiter returning to its place in her birthchart, there were other aspects being made. For example, Pluto at that time was conjunct Jupiter, and Mars had moved to conjunct her Moon. Astrology identifies important times in your life through a build-up of many aspects at one time. A single transiting aspect can go by almost unnoticed, but when there are several, that reflects the energy of big events.

By 1981, Madonna had already developed much of the mystique that was to propel her to stardom in music and movies. During that period she shot the second part of the movie *Certain Sacrifice*, which wasn't released until 1985. Reviewers said it was terrible. This was one of those instances where an opportunity was grasped, but it turned out to be a poor choice. By the time of Jupiter's third return, Madonna had hit the charts in both the music and movie industries, showing she was able to learn from experience and move on.

Exercise

To learn more about important processes in your life, examine Jupiter and its aspects in your birthchart.

1. Find the sign Jupiter occupies. Consider its element and mode, and how expansion and function work there.

2. What house does Jupiter occupy? This shows the area of life where you expand your awareness on the physical, emotional, mental, and spiritual levels.

3. List Jupiter's aspects. Think about the relationships formed, based on the planets and the various aspects.

4. Consider how you can boost the energy of each aspect, or how you can modify the energy if it is out of control.

Summary

We have seen how Jupiter reflects function and process on the physical and other levels of experience. We have also looked at the Ninth House, the area of the chart associated with Jupiter, and we have considered the sextile aspect as it relates to the opportunities we find in life.

Now we turn to Saturn. Function follows form, and form follows function. Saturn reflects structure in our lives. Jupiter and Saturn team up to reflect our lives at every stage of development.

10
Saturn, the Tenth House, and the Semisquare and Sesquisquare

Astrologer Paul Grell, in his book *Keywords*, captures the essence of the more traditional view of Saturn. He states that "Father Saturn's goal is *perfection*."[1] Then he goes on to list all the trials Saturn brings into our lives in order to teach us "experience, patience, humility, wisdom and compassion."[2] Saturn, basically, is seen as the reflection of all of life's most difficult lessons, in the hope that we learn and grow to become confident, dependable individuals.

There is another view of Saturn. Just as I believe that there are no "bad" signs, I also believe that no planet is better or worse than another—they are each *different*. Thus I feel we must look at each planet from a less judgmental perspective, considering the basic energy both for its creative expression and its less constructive expression.

Structure, Not Limitation

Saturn is the most distant planet in our solar system visible to the naked eye. It therefore defines a limit of sorts, yet we know there is more—at least three planets more that we have seen through telescopes and visited through mechanical probes. The balance point defines human intelligence and intelligent activity. Science, one expression of our intelligence, has provided the means to see beyond the limit of Saturn's orbit to other members of the solar system.

The basic functional property of Saturn relates to structure. Structure can be understood in terms of the physical, mental, emotional, and spiritual content of our lives.

Physical

Bones, teeth, hair, skin. As we read these four words, we notice ways in which we truly appreciate the value of structure. Without bones we could not stand upright and walk. Without teeth we could not eat a wide variety of foods. Hair adorns our bodies and skin provides a very sensible limit—it holds us together. In addition to these obvious bodily structures, Saturn indicates how we relate to the structure of the world at large. Saturn is associated with massive structures like hills and mountains, and also large buildings and other humanmade structures.

Mental

Systematic learning of facts. Saturn reflects our capacity to concentrate on a specific subject and to gather information about it. As we learn, we develop self-discipline, another Saturn association. Other Saturn thought-to-action processes include responsibility, attention to duty, patience, and diplomacy.

Emotional

Experiential learning and judgment. Each experience in our lives provides us with the material we need to develop sound judgment. Judgment is felt in the body. It is largely a feeling assessment of the validity of the information we have available. For example, most medicines taste bad. Our first judgment is, "Not pleasant! Take it away!" Yet we learn to associate medicine with healing. We use what patience we have to test its efficacy. If we get positive results within a time frame dictated by our patience, then we judge it to be effective. In a future situation we may be more willing to try another medicine. This willingness is a judgment that has an emotional basis.

The same sort of thing applies to evaluating relationships with other people, engaging in the world through education and vocation, etc. We develop our judgment capacity through experience, and we judge on a feeling or emotional basis in concert with logical evaluation.

Spiritual

Karma. First let's define karma and dharma. Some people relate karma to the past, as the result of past actions, and dharma to the future, where work and general life direction are concerned. Saturn fits both of these definitions. As Chronos, Saturn is called the Lord of Time. This planet is a key to vocational success and is therefore an essential consideration where the future is involved.

Karma is the result of the past, and dharma is the direction of the future. Both are integrally involved with the concept of choice. We made choices and we now see the results in our lives. That's karma. As we make better, more informed choices, we set the direction of our work and plant the seeds of future results.

Wisdom expresses in every area of daily life. We all make the best choices we can. However, through study and consideration, our personal "best" is improved. Wisdom is the application of what we know to a situation. It incorporates the capacity to seek additional facts to inform our decisions. The better informed the decision, the better our work, and the better our future karma may be.

Saturn's energy is reflected in a broad range of life experiences. Some of our experiences are judged to be "bad" and some "good." Saturn's energy is neither good nor bad, but rather it is structured. As we grow and learn, we develop stability. We also develop a systematic approach to the world, and this approach is framed within a structure of physical, mental, emotional, and spiritual understanding.

Saturn Through the Signs

Saturn in Aries

Saturn in Aries reflects a modesty that may be missing from Aries otherwise. A sense of self-restraint is evident. The will is strong, but not as uncontrolled as with other planets in Aries. There is a tendency to act on your own, and this can be a problem when what is needed is cooperation. The most positive attributes are ambition and endurance.

Saturn in Taurus

The perseverance of Saturn in Taurus is not the same as Aries endurance. With Saturn here you are able to follow through, even in cases where you wonder if you can endure it. Method is part of your makeup. You are able to acquire material things, build a career, or sustain a relationship because you apply yourself day by day to the task. At times, though, forward movement is imperceptibly slow.

Saturn in Gemini

Thorough thought and work are hallmarks of this placement of Saturn. There is not great endurance, and this can manifest as a lack of adaptability to difficult situations. However, the capacity to think through to a good solution often overcomes limitations.

Saturn in Cancer

There is either a strong emotional control or a hypersensitivity that leads to emotional extremes. Difficult childhood relationships may color your feelings about other people who seem to take on the characteristics of your parents. You love your own independence and like to maintain some reserve around other people.

Saturn in Leo

Saturn here reflects reliability and loyalty. You may rise to a position of responsibility because of these two traits, both of which are much valued in the vocational realm. Formality can produce strain for you, though. Shyness colors all interpersonal relationships and may inhibit sexual expression.

Saturn in Virgo

This placement of Saturn reflects meticulous attention to accuracy and detail. Correctness is valued over enthusiasm. At best you are serious. At worst you take a pedantic approach to interactions with others. You may find that you are understood best when you lighten up and let go of your desire for perfection, in yourself and in others.

Saturn in Libra

If you cultivate the spirit of cooperation, the strength of Saturn in Libra comes through, and you develop lasting partnerships in business and marriage. Because you tend to maintain a distance between yourself and others, you often appear to be discontented. The longer a relationship lasts, the better able you will be to relax and enjoy your partner.

Saturn in Scorpio

Saturn in Scorpio is often reflected as stubbornness. You are able to plumb the depths of any subject, and this can be seen as a stubborn attachment to an idea instead of as a positive trait. You may pursue metaphysical subjects. Your contribution to the world will very likely come through your determined pursuits that lead to your spiritual rebirth.

Saturn in Sagittarius

Your firm grasp of concepts like justice and prudence is strong. However, what you see in the world around you may cause you to want to be somewhere else. This can lead to a desire to emigrate, or at least to move far from your birthplace. You gravitate toward religious and philosophical studies, which help alleviate doubts that arise.

Saturn in Capricorn

Saturn is comfortable in this sign, so slow advancement through concentrated effort may be an adequate payoff for your efforts in your career. Your narrow focus, however, can lead to a somewhat one-sided view of life. To balance your egocentric nature, you can consciously develop and use the energy of other planets in your chart.

Saturn in Aquarius

Your strong ideals provide a defined path through life. You attract others to your cause, and may form strong relationships. This is good, as a friend can provide restraint for your sometimes overly ambitious plans. Without this moderating influence you may be disappointed in the results you obtain.

Saturn in Pisces

The strength of Saturn in Pisces is a modest attitude toward life. You are able to work in seclusion, and may even prefer it to the hustle and bustle of the office or social arena. Generally, though, you need contact with other people to keep your hand in various activities. This way you are less lonely.

The Saturn Cycle

We saw in the previous chapter that the Jupiter cycle focuses on development in childhood and throughout your adult life. While the main focus of attention was Jupiter's return to its degree in the birthchart, mention was made of the fact that the phases of Jupiter's cycles—the halfway point in particular—sometimes coincide with significant points in the Saturn cycle.

Because the Saturn cycle is longer—about twenty-eight to thirty years in length—we will consider the quarter and halfway points in greater detail. These all indicate significant milestones in both child and adult development.

Physical Development

Because Saturn reflects structure, the development of strong bones and teeth is significant. The maintenance of healthy skin, bones, and teeth remains important right up to the end of life, so it is no small consideration. At about the time Saturn has moved through one sign, or about two and one-half years, a child is usually standing and walking. The skull has knit together, providing protection for the head and brain. The child has a set of baby teeth. Thus the first years of life set the tone for the future where physical ability is concerned.

Intellectual Development

By the time Saturn has reached the first square to its position at age seven to seven and one-half, the child is usually in school. More intellectual development occurs in the first seven and one-half year period than in the entire rest of one's life. The capacity to communicate verbally provides the foundation for all learning, rational thought, and later emotional and spiritual development as well. This phase marks the time when we realize that actions are associated with results in a direct manner, and thus we are responsible for our own actions.

Emotional Development

By the time Saturn reaches the opposite point in the zodiac at around age fourteen to fifteen, we have entered puberty and are wrestling with emotional developmental issues. We have friends outside the family group and are influenced by their ideas. We are challenged to manage physical changes in our bodies that cause an emotional uproar, and at the same time we reach a new plateau of intellectual development, where we are capable of abstract thinking. This is when we begin to understand that not all things in our lives are limited to a cause-and-effect relationship.

Productivity

By the time Saturn has reached the second square on its return toward the birth position, we are generally well into the pursuit of some productive vocation. At age twenty-one, we may not have completed college. However, college is a foundation for all future productivity, and can been seen as a major work effort—we employ our minds to learn about the world and about our desired vocational field. If we are not in college, we have entered the adult world and may have a job, a marriage partner, and even small children to raise.

Spiritual Development

At about age twenty-eight to thirty, when Saturn has completed its first journey around the birthchart, we are well into the productive period of our lives. We may have had a full-time job for some time, and we may also have school-age children. We now face a moment when we reap the results of the first third of our lives. The Saturn Return is well-known to astrologers as a time when we feel the "crunch" of adulthood. Like any conjunction, when Saturn conjuncts its birth position we often set out in new directions.

Not the least of the new directions is an intense review of our spiritual beliefs. We may reevaluate our religious and philosophical values, and often we find them not as fulfilling as we would like. During the entire second Saturn cycle, one purpose of our lives is to find those beliefs and activities that prove to be satisfying for the long haul. In the process we give up some of what we were taught, learn new things, and restructure our vocational and social paths to suit our new or renewed ideals.

Saturn continues to travel through our chart. The second circuit comprises the bulk of the productive period of life, both biological and vocational. At the second Saturn Return at around age fifty-six to sixty, we prepare for the final period of our lives, during which we may pursue yet another vocational path, and during which we consolidate our intellectual and spiritual beliefs. If our initial physical development was strong, we have the potential to live for many more years.

The Tenth House

In the same way that the Ascendant is not the same as the First House, the Midheaven is different from the Tenth House. (See chapter 15 for more information on the Midheaven.) The Midheaven is the point on the ecliptic that is the highest in the sky at the time of birth. In the tropics the Midheaven may be directly overhead, at the point called the Zenith. The Tenth House is the segment of the chart immediately to the east of the Midheaven. It is the part of the chart that next rises to the Midheaven. The Sun is in the Tenth House from about 10:00 to 12:00 in the morning. The Tenth House represents the most public and prominent part of our lives. Two areas of life that fit this description are career and social status.

Family position often defines social position. Two children born at the same time into different social situations will have very different lives. There is a story about a king of England who had an identical "twin" whose father operated an ordinary business. While the king traveled in the most elite social circles, his twin was at the top of his social circle as well. It was a very different circle, but he also reached the top. As children we usually don't have much choice about social position. As adults we can change our social position through our work, through marriage, and through other choices.

Career is a matter of the Tenth House. The sign on the cusp of this house and the planets here describe the most obvious course of your career. Usually there is part of a second sign, and sometimes even a third, in the Tenth House, and these may indicate second or third career possibilities. If you don't have any planets in the Tenth House, this does not mean that you won't have a career. It means that career matters are related to another part of the chart. What you do is look for the planet that is normally associated with the sign on the Midheaven. Then find the house that planet is in. This house and matters associated with it have a major effect on your career.

When you think about career and the Tenth House, think about the broad career fields associated with the signs. Each field has many roles and can accommodate different educational levels, creative talents, and emotional desires. Remember that career fields overlap. Thus a medical technician will use computers, and a computer programmer may write medical programs. Planets in the Tenth House and aspects to the planet associated with the Tenth-House sign often indicate the actual job you pursue within the broader career field.

- **Aries**—Adventure, fire department, metallurgy, military, physical therapy
- **Taurus**—Acting, cabinetry and furniture, geology, hospitality, banking or finance

- **Gemini**—Accounting, driving a vehicle, writing, editing, librarian, translator, office worker
- **Cancer**—Agriculture, boats, fishing, housekeeping, merchant, dairy, plumbing, social work
- **Leo**—Sporting goods, goldsmith, government, investment banking, the theater
- **Virgo**—Administration, training, healer, mathematics, nanny, office worker, veterinary services
- **Libra**—Acting, arbitration, courthouses, negotiation, sales, sociologist, decorating
- **Scorpio**—Druggist, doctor, insurance, magic, mortuaries, psychiatry, psychic, surgery
- **Sagittarius**—Advertising, airlines, attorney, foreign policy, teaching, publishing, religion
- **Capricorn**—Administrator, ambassador, governor, industrial engineering, real estate, vocational counselor
- **Aquarius**—Airplane mechanic, astrology, psychotherapy, radiology, telephone systems
- **Pisces**—Artist, astrologer, dancer, distilling, oceanographer, prisons, secret service, weaver

The Semisquare and Sesquisquare Aspect

Saturn relates to function on both the external physical plane and the internal mental plan. Two aspects define the activities of planets on an internal level: the semisquare (∠) and sesquisquare (⊡) (also called sesquiquadrate) aspects are halfway between the conjunction and square, or the square and opposition. They are 45 and 135 degrees, respectively. The other aspects we have examined so far all came in 30 degree units, and thus were predictably connected with signs of similar element or mode. The conjunction relates two planets in the same sign, the square and opposition have planets in the same mode, the trine connects planets in the same element, and the sextile links compatible elements.

Both the semisquare and sesquisquare have planets in signs of a different mode and element. This means that any comfortable connection we have seen in the aspects so far is missing. Right away we can sense the tension in such an aspect. Because the more obvious compatible connection to the world is missing, these aspects are internalized. Because they are internalized, you feel their energy very strongly, but other people do not perceive that energy in you. This leads to a lot of misunderstanding of what you are thinking and feeling. You have to explain yourself where these aspects are concerned. In fact, you often have to explain to yourself, too.

Consider the phases of the Moon. It is fairly easy to understand the New, quarter, and Full Moon positions. The New Moon is similar to the conjunction, in that it represents a moment for new beginnings. The quarters of the Moon relate to the square aspect, where our energy is moving and we sometimes challenge ourselves to get things accomplished. The Full Moon is similar to the opposition aspect, where we become aware of significant events or emotional conditions in our lives.

But what about the in-between phases of the Moon? When we look at the Moon, we can see how close it is to New, quarter, or Full. Yet we may feel slightly off balance when the moon is in between phases. It seems to be neither new nor full, nor halfway between. There is no solid feeling we can identify. Something similar occurs with the semisquare and sesquisquare aspects.

These aspects reflect in our lives in the form of tension, insecurity, irritation, or agitation. Here's an example of how the semisquare and sesquisquare work. If you have the Sun and Mars in square aspect, you see their activities clearly in events and situations. You are able to identify yourself in relation to energies around you. With the semisquare it's different. You feel the tension of the energy, but you may find you cannot identify it. You are irritated and anxious, but you are not sure why. With the sesquisquare, in my experience, the feeling is more of agitation. You feel metaphorically like you are inside a washing machine, with the machine making things happen. You don't understand the mechanism; you only feel its effect. The people around you wonder why you are upset. They are usually totally unaware of what is bothering you.

These aspects indicate areas of your life where you are likely to run into tension or agitation again and again. They are unsettling parts of your life. As you learn through experience, you become better at telling other people what you are feeling, and you gain understanding of the effects of the planets in such an aspect when they are trying to work together. Tension is often the source of a lot of creative energy. Your desire to resolve stress leads to creative results.

Case Study: Ted Turner

Ted Turner has several semisquare and sesquisquare aspects. The closest aspects in his chart are Moon semisquare Ascendant, and Sun sesquisquare Saturn. Venus also forms a sesquisquare to Saturn.

Lois Rodden, on her AstroDatabank website, states that Ted Turner "was raised by his dad to view insecurity as the secret of success."[3] From the discussion of the semisquare and sesquisquare, it is easy to imagine having feelings of insecurity with these aspects. Gwenda Blair, writing in *Business Monthly*, stated about Ted Turner: "The man who looks like Clark Gable and sounds like Huey Long has been an unpredictable joker in the cable industry—and in the American psyche. He built a communications empire by taking enormous risks, always flouting the conventional wisdom."[4] What makes him unpredictable? The semisquare and sesquisquare aspects help answer this question.

The Moon semisquare Ascendant indicates that Ted's personal relationships with other people are fraught with hypersensitivity. He becomes annoyed with other people largely because they cannot discern his inner feelings, which to him are self-apparent. He comes across as expecting other people to be there for him all the time. Ted is an intelligent man. One suspects that he logically understands this is not reasonable, yet he continues to demand it of others.

The Sun sesquisquare Saturn suggests an internal struggle. Saturn in Aries is ambitious, and the Sun in Scorpio is driven by the will to succeed. The agitation of the sesquisquare aspect suggests that Ted feels the drives strongly but may misunderstand them. His sense of responsibility is reflected in massive cash donations to the United Nations and the work of his own foundation to improve the environment. The Sun in Scorpio may overestimate his emotional stamina from time to time. Thus the agitation of this aspect, while it drives him to succeed, may also cause breakdowns in communication, and also physical strain almost to the breaking point.

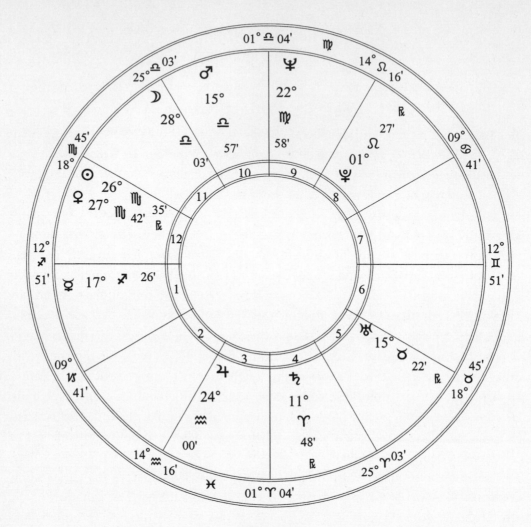

Chart 19

Ted Turner

November 19, 1938 / Cincinnati, OH / 8:50 A.M. EST

Koch Houses

Exercise

Using your own chart, take a look at the dynamics of Saturn.

1. What sign does Saturn occupy? What does it indicate about how you connect with the world around you?

2. What house is Saturn in? What does that tell you about structure, responsibility, and other Saturn-related topics?

3. Saturn's aspects indicate supporting or challenging factors. List them and indicate how each shows something about structure in your life.

4. Find the semisquare and sesquisquare aspects in your chart. What are the tensions and stresses you feel?

5. Summarize your findings: How do you approach responsibilities? What kind of structure are you looking for? How do you handle the stresses involved?

Now consider the Tenth House in your chart. This will indicate the careers or career fields you find attractive.

6. What is the sign on the cusp of the Tenth House? Think about careers that suit the energy of this sign.

7. What planets are in the Tenth House? These will indicate associates in the career field.

8. Look at the sign on the Midheaven and the next sign. Which planets are usually associated with these signs? Where are these planets (in which houses)? Think about how these other houses relate to your career focus (activities).

Now see how the Saturn indications align with the career indications.

9. Does your picture of structure and responsibility seem like it lines up with your career indicators?

10. Does the stress level in the chart feel consistent with the indicated career fields?

11. Do you notice other aspects in the chart that seem more important than the semisquares and sesquisquares? How do the aspects you have read about so far influence what you think about the semisquares?

Summary

Your view of structure in your life, particularly where career is concerned, is very important to your overall success. Internal stress, as measured by the semisquare and sesquisquare aspects, is one way to measure your degree of satisfaction in all areas of life, including career. We saw with Saturn that structure is a good thing in our lives. Some stress is also normal. Physicians talk about good stress, which builds physical and cardio-vascular strength, versus bad stress (excessive anxiety and worry), which is not healthy.

Now that we have explored all the planets in the visible portion of our solar system, we turn to the outer, or transpersonal, planets: Uranus, Neptune, and Pluto. These planets indicate how we use our extrasensory abilities to understand the world. They also indicate areas where we need to learn new ways of communicating with the people around us.

---

1. Paul Grell, *Keywords* (Washington: American Federation of Astrologers, 1970) 7.

2. Ibid.

3. See www.astrodatabank.com.

4. See abcnews.go.com/reference/bios/turner.html.

11
Uranus, the Eleventh House, and the Semisextile and Quincunx

It is my opinion that the most significant quality of Uranus is equilibrium. Throughout human history, the gods associated with Uranus have been responsible for restoring equilibrium to the world and their actions take on new significance when viewed from this perspective.

In Shakespeare's plays, for example, the balance among individual, Body Politic, and universal spheres was considered to be of great importance. Whenever actions of individuals or larger social events put the times "out of joint," balance was restored through sometimes cataclysmic events. Lady Macbeth's greed, for example, was redressed only after a number of cosmic signs were observed, and after a war.

Uranus has numerous moons and rings similar to Saturn. Uranus has five major moons. Two were discovered by Herschel in 1787 and were named Oberon and Titania, after Shakespearean characters. Lassell discovered Ariel and Umbriel in 1851, and named them after the spirits in Alexander Pope's poem "The Rape of the Lock." Miranda (another Shakespearean name) was discovered by Kuiper in 1948.

The orbit of Uranus is remarkably stable, with an eccentricity of only 0.047. Uranus' path around the Sun is more uniform than that of Mercury, Mars, Jupiter, Saturn, or Pluto. The greatest latitude Uranus achieves is approximately 0 degrees 46 minutes (in 1927). This means that Uranus' orbit is very close to the ecliptic. It compares with Mercury at 7 degrees, the Moon at 5 degrees, and Pluto at 16 degrees.

To review, the key principle for the delineation of Jupiter was function; that for Saturn was structure. For Uranus, the principle of equilibrium is a central focus. Time after time, clients have complained about a loss of equilibrium during Uranus transits, yet Uranus' role is actually to reestablish balance.

Relating to Uranus, astrologers use terms like suddenness, revolution, and change. Yet the biological correspondence of Uranus to rhythm carries through to all areas of expression, and there is a point of equilibrium within all rhythmic movement. We complain of sudden events in our lives sometimes, but we usually have had the opportunity to become aware of trends as they develop. In cases where we have *not* become aware, it is often because we have refused to see what was right before our eyes. I recall a friend who said her husband changed "overnight" when Uranus transited his Ascendant. Another woman underwent radical relationship changes each time Uranus conjoined a natal planet. These events were described as "sudden" changes or impulses, yet outsiders had seen the problems coming for some time.

When people describe their intuitive capacity, they are describing a Uranian process. We get feelings, visions, and other information over a period of time. Then suddenly we "get it." Something happens and all the pieces fall into place. The pivotal event seems sudden, but the chain of intuitive insights occurred over a period of time. The impact—the realization—comes suddenly and resolves misunderstandings or inconsistencies in our thoughts.

As we cultivate the inner vision or voice of intuition, we become more skilled at listening. Our feelings become more meaningful as we observe them and work with them. Our dreams present clearer pictures of the inner self and its message, matching our intuition about the outer world. We also develop ways to test intuitive information as we go along, instead of waiting for flashes of insight that previously were connected with apparently sudden events.

People actually have different styles of intuition. Presented in this light, the interplay of energies offers insight into different intuitive potentials. By focusing on intuition and the judgment that results, we will develop a view of life that is unique to the planet Uranus.

In reviewing the tales in which fairies and sprites play active roles in human events, I wonder whether Shakespeare and Pope actually believed in such beings. Certainly Shakespeare played upon the beliefs of his audience when he made a ghost appear to Hamlet, or witches to MacBeth. Pope used the characters of Ariel and Umbriel for satirical purposes, and his audience most assuredly recognized the satire. Yet both audiences were asked to put aside whatever disbelief they had for the duration of the play or poem. In spite of doubt about the existence of the fairies and sprites whose names grace Uranus' moons, the characters express the nature of intuition and equilibrium associated with Uranus.

Before the first scene of Shakespeare's *The Tempest*, Miranda and her father, the deposed duke of Milan, had been shipwrecked on an island. Thus, from the first moment of the play, there is a need to bring the social sphere back into equilibrium. The only human character to give a name to Uranus' moons, Miranda embodies the feminine quality of space; she also signifies the human quality. We become comfortable with the changes indicated by Uranus when we cultivate intuitive understanding of the rhythms and cycles of the solar system and of the universe.

Romance

The role of Uranian energy in love relationships should not be overlooked by the astrologer. This makes perfect sense when we recognize the importance of ceremony and ritual in our interpersonal relationships. Uranus provides the ritual boundaries within which relationships grow. Moreover, it can show where an imbalance is likely to occur, providing us with the conscious ground upon which to learn life's lessons.

The transits of Uranus bring new people into our lives. When Uranus forms aspects to the birth Venus, we often meet partners who remain significant to us for years. These meetings are often big surprises—we may not be seeking a new relationship at all.

Intuition

Intuition allows us to reach beyond our personal sense of balance toward a larger experience of equilibrium. The orbit of Uranus is never more than 1 degree away from that of the ecliptic; this reflects a metaphorical balance between the Earth and Uranus. For example, ritual allows us to communicate between the inner self and the outer world, to gain a sense of proper action, and to communicate between the ordinary human senses and the spiritual realm. It is interesting to note that communicating with the macrocosm by going out from the self is not that different from going inward—the initial effort only seems different. Communication occurs on three levels:

- Language is the vehicle for communication between one person and another. While it may not be completely precise in terms of feelings or intuition, or even in terms of sensation, language forms the pattern of our thinking, and it allows us to communicate with one another relatively clearly.

- Your ego complex has its own language, learned in early childhood. It has its own structure and symbolism. It draws upon the collective mind and thus has much in common with other people, but each person has his or her own unique complex of language forms that permit communication.

- The third category, communication with the universe by going outward, has a similar language, although it is often experienced through feelings or sensations, without the benefit of words. It is a "knowing" that does not really depend on words. The mechanism involved is one of opening to the broader possibility. It is paradoxical that the void we identify by going inward is really no different from the vastness of space that we experience by going outward.

Change

Uranus reflects sudden and abrupt change on the physical level, intuition on the mental level, and rhythm on the biological level. As astrologers, we study the movement of Uranus and experience the sudden changes it can signal. We have each had the opportunity to establish our own rhythm when we experience Uranian changes in our lives. Such a personal rhythm will manifest itself again and again.

Intuition is often experienced as a rather sudden understanding, yet upon examination we realize that we have been gaining understanding over an extended period of time. The moment when we say "Aha!" is only the moment when we grasp what we have been learning. Usually the learning does not all take place in one particular instant.

Rhythm, as the biological correspondent, is the inward and outward movement of the breath, the opening and closing of chambers of the heart, the pulsing of blood through the system. All the rhythms of the body, brain wave patterns, galvanic skin response—anything that embodies the outward movement of impulse and the inward movement of response in the body—is part of the Uranian rhythm. In the birthchart, Uranus aspects often indicate times when the rhythm is upset. We experience these upsets as happening rather suddenly, but in general most of them have been upcoming events that, if we have cultivated awareness, we would have been able to identify.

Events, then, seem to happen suddenly, while actually there is a cyclical movement of energy beforehand. Uranus moves very slowly through the zodiac, and yet is seen as the signal of sudden action. Chapter 14 explains in detail how transiting aspects work in the birthchart. Usually there is an aspect of an outer planet, followed by aspects from faster-moving planets to activate the energy. Because a planet like Uranus moves so slowly, the energy has been onstage, so to speak, for a long time, and needs a faster-moving planet to activate it—to initiate dialogue. In actuality, the energies necessary for the event have been a long time in coming and we had opportunities to foresee them.

Uranus and Astrology

Many astrologers have Uranus prominently placed in their chart. This planet therefore has a remarkable influence over the individual astrologer's life.

The Sun transits the zodiac in one year; Uranus transits the Sun in eighty-four years. The Uranian cycle is far longer than the apparent geocentric cycle. As astrologers we know that this eighty-four-year cycle of Uranus has a profound effect on our human life. As it is moving through the twelve signs, the energy of Uranus is shifting from one area of life to another.

The placement of Uranus itself in the birthchart will help us understand our own intuition, as well as the best use of Uranian energy in assisting others in their search for balance. Once we have examined the placement of Uranus, we get a broader picture of what we can do with that energy in our lives.

- We cooperate from the perspective of balance, instead of from a personal, petty viewpoint. Understanding the mental power available through this transpersonal planet can show us a way to shift the focus of our mental energy from something that has been not quite satisfactory to something that is more completely productive and creative.

- Our experience of revelation is reflected in Uranus in the geocentric chart. We can look at the birthchart to understand how each individual understands it in a slightly different way. Uranus shows us a lot about how we gain that understanding.

- Understanding ourselves within our roles in ritual behavior can be understood by examining the position of Uranus in the birthchart as well.

Uranus Through the Signs

Uranus in Aries (1927–1934, 2010–2018)

The suddenness of Uranus, combined with the impulsiveness of Aries, suggests the potential of too much energy deploying too quickly. There may be bursts of energetic action, followed by a stubborn insistence that one's actions have been proper. The strength of this combination lies in the intuitive grasp of situations. Thus, while your actions may seem abrupt, they are often based on positive intuitive insights. You know the right thing to do, and you don't hesitate to do it.

Uranus in Taurus (1934–1941, 2018–2025)

Your intuition reaches profound depths with Uranus in Taurus. Your awareness comes from a connection to the planet itself. You are very resourceful because you understand the flow of energy, whether it is along financial or other material lines. There is a tendency to put all your eggs in one basket, and this can be risky even in the best of times. Unlike Uranus in Aries, you are well advised to wait patiently for the right moment to take action.

Uranus in Gemini (1941–1948, 2025–2032)

Uranus is associated with an air sign (Aquarius), so it is comfortable in Gemini. The combination of strong intuition and strong intellect provides the basis for a successful educational career. The same skills are beneficial in many career fields where one must project far into the future. Mental energy can be scattered, leaving you without the results you seek. Still, your original ideas make your life stimulating and interesting.

Uranus in Cancer (1948–1955, 2032–2039)

With Uranus in the sign of Cancer, intuition is coupled with a feeling sense that may even provide psychic sensitivity. You are able to understand others well, and this can lead to unusual friendships and associations. You tend to resist family and cultural lessons, and instead may gravitate toward groups very unlike your ancestors, or even move to another country. Your powerful memory serves you well, but you have to cultivate it.

Uranus in Leo (1871–1878, 1955 1961)

You are bold. I could stop with this remark, as it is the hallmark of Uranus in Leo. Your boldness, however, can lead you into either positive or destructive activities. On the one hand you love a good adventure and cannot satisfy this side of your personality merely by watching movies. On the other hand, you may be a powerful leader, and you need to take a bit of responsibility if you want your followers to trust you. You are more successful when you resist gambling on uncertain outcomes.

Uranus in Virgo (1878–1884, 1961–1968)

Intuition and practical application are attributes of this combination. However, because sensation and intuition are opposite functions, according to Carl Jung, one of them is less conscious, resulting in uneven expression of one or the other. If sensation is less conscious, then you are apt to be overly severe and critical of others. If intuition is less conscious, your associates cannot depend on your insights on a consistent basis. This placement of Uranus, then, will need cultivation to bring it to its full potential.

Uranus in Libra (1884–1890, 1968–1974)

As with Gemini, the combination of intuition and intellect is strong with Uranus in Libra, but you are not as adaptable. Your deeply felt sense of the balance and harmony around you can provide a beacon for others who are less sensitive to the group energy. Your desire to direct the energy of a situation can label you as a troublemaker, largely because other people never quite understand why you want to go in a particular direction.

Uranus in Scorpio (1890–1897, 1974–1981)

You are very responsive on the energetic level and may be capable of physical healing. Your intuition can lead you into trouble when you fearlessly rush into situations and forget to heed due caution. As you learn to work with your abundance of energy, you learn to consider options logically instead of making hasty changes. Training your intuitive talents is necessary, as you have them from childhood and may not know what to do with them.

Uranus in Sagittarius (1897–1904, 1981–1988)

You see beyond the surface of religious rituals to the deeper connection to the universe. You also see past people's actions to their deeper intentions. Your own desire for adventure and change guides your life. The associated restlessness can keep you from developing long-lasting relationships and a career path. It is helpful for you to align your strong intuitive capacity with your sense of structure (indicated by Saturn's placement). Then you have a firm base from which to pursue your ideas and ideals.

Uranus in Capricorn (1904–1912, 1988–1995)

If you are looking at a chart with this placement, it is the chart of a child or someone over ninety years old. Uranus in Capricorn indicates concentrated energy that can be directed toward ambitious goals. Technical aptitude may combine with education to provide a wonderful career potential. Your capacity to concentrate on a goal is due in part to the fact that you don't intuit the end result, but visualize how to reach it. Aristotle Onassis had this placement, as did Ronald Reagan and Lyndon Johnson.

Uranus in Aquarius (1912–1919, 1995–2003)

At the time of this writing, Uranus is in Aquarius. Eighty years ago Uranus was in Aquarius when Jonas Salk, developer of the polio vaccine, was born. Other ingenious people with this placement include William Burroughs, Red Skelton, and Richard Nixon. A theme for this generation was the understanding of human nature. There was a rebellious quality that sometimes led to trouble, and sometimes led to great success. Burroughs and Nixon, for example, both did things that were well beyond the limits of legality, yet both left a legacy in their respective fields. We can expect children being born at the present time to be capable of progressive change in society, medicine, and other fields.

Uranus in Pisces (1919–1927, 2003–2010)

Strongly inclined to mysticism, Uranus in Pisces is attuned to the subconscious forces around us. You have a powerful capacity for healing, but people will not be aware of it unless you tell them. Your intentions may be misunderstood and your mysterious tendencies make you seem unreliable. People with Uranus in Pisces include David Brinkley, Ray Bradbury, and Timothy Leary, as well as Lauren Bacall, Queen Elizabeth of England, and Marilyn Monroe.

The Eleventh House

Uranus is the planet closely associated with Aquarius, and the natural placement for Aquarius is the Eleventh House. The Eleventh House reflects the shins, calves, and ankles. These parts of the body are integrally related to our ability to move around in our environment. The connection to the world around us is made moment to moment by our movements, so the strength and flexibility of our legs is central to our capacity to engage in the world. If we are severely limited, we may have mechanical aids such as motorized wheelchairs that reflect our technical ingenuity.

At the same time, the Eleventh House reflects areas of our lives that are outside the sphere of personal control. Friends and other associates, particularly groups of other people, are indicated by the sign and planets here. We know that individuals have the capacity to think through situations and make personal decisions, but we have also seen the capacity for crowds of people to be swayed in directions they would normally not take.

Often we find that situations and events of the Eleventh House involve circumstances beyond our control. Mass transit is an example where we must take on faith the mechanical reliability of the vehicle and the skill of the driver or pilot. If you are not the pilot of the plane, you are not in control. If you did not check out the condition of the brakes on the bus, you are not certain of their mechanical condition. If you are not the only car on the road, you are subject to the actions of others. There are endless examples where we exercise faith in people and situations.

Finally, hopes and wishes are reflected here. As the house opposite the Fifth House, the Eleventh House indicates the love and creative energy of others, and therefore the love we receive from others. We are in control of our own future in many ways, but the Eleventh House is concerned primarily with the times when we are not. We hope that things work out the best way possible in all those instances, and we depend on the goodwill of people and the universe itself. The Eleventh House shows how we accept this role.

The Semisextile and Quincunx Aspects

Continuing the theme of equilibrium, or lack of it, let's consider the semisextile and quincunx aspects. These two aspects have only come into common use recently. The traditional aspect group used by Claudius Ptolemy includes only aspects that divide the 360 degree circle by one, two, three, and four—the conjunction, opposition, trine, and square. Along with the sextile, discussed in chapter 9, the semisextile and quincunx complete the group of aspects that consist of even 30 degree units. The semisextile is 30 degrees and the quincunx, also called the inconjunct, is 150 degrees. Both aspects involve the capacity to expand our activities, as well as the adjustments necessary as we do so. The semisextile aspect lacks balance because it is not quite conjunct. The quincunx is imbalanced because it is not quite opposite.

The semisextile reflects growth in the chart, but this growth often has some pain attached to it. The feeling is that of a beautiful rose and has the attendant "thorns." On the one hand, we experience growth and expansion, building a foundation for our future. We make progress through our own efforts. On the other hand, we face circumstances in our lives that provoke us to grow and change. Events impel us to expand our minds and try new things.

The quincunx, in contrast, often impels us to work too hard to get what we want. We become immersed in details and may fail to see the broader picture. We miss the clarity of awareness that is associated with the opposition. Overwork can lead to illness when we strain our physical systems beyond their capacity. Other people may expect us to go longer and do more than we would choose. Events tend to pile up on us, until we feel "buried" in our work. The quincunx aspect is often active when people leave us through separation or death. The house placement of the planets in the quincunx usually indicates something about the person who leaves.

Generally speaking, both of these aspects involve elements of adjacent signs. For example, a planet in Aries typically forms a semisextile to a planet in Pisces or Taurus, and a quincunx to a planet in Virgo or Scorpio. These aspects have a lack of compatibility built into them, as the planets involved fall in different elements *and* different modes. This explains the undertone of friction involved. Even when the aspect indicates movement in a logical direction through the zodiac, as the semisextile does, the movement requires a total change of mentality if it is to work—hence the demand for adjustment reflected in these two aspects. The semisextile is growth through pain (remember the

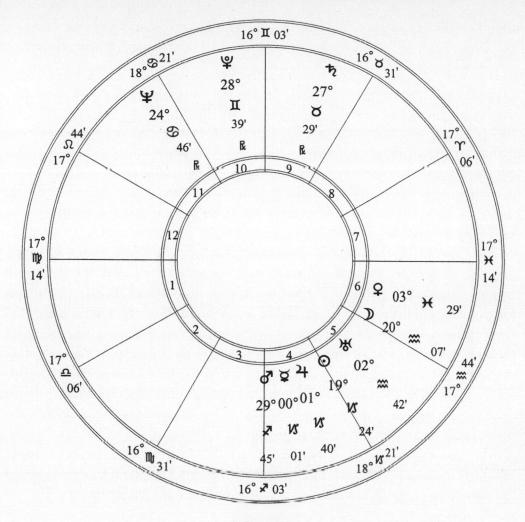

Chart 20
Richard Nixon
January 9, 1913 / Whittier, CA / 9:35 P.M. PST
Koch Houses

thorns on the desired roses) and adjustment (you adjust to others and to your own capabilities). The quincunx can indicate a physical adjustment through illness or injury, or an emotional adjustment to people and situations.

Case Study: Richard Nixon

Richard Nixon was a powerful political figure who changed the face of international politics by seeking out a relationship with China. This single act provided him with a permanent place in history, as it was a necessary yet bold and determined act. From a position of profound anti-Communist mentality, Nixon engaged in diplomatic efforts to bring China into the world of international politics at a time when world tensions were at an unendurable level of strain.

The capacity for creative decision making and action is shown by Uranus in Aquarius in the Fifth House. Aspects in his chart include the Sun semisextile the Moon, and Uranus semisextile Jupiter and Mercury in Capricorn and Mars in Sagittarius. Uranus forms a semisextile to Venus in Pisces. The potential for innovation in his career was clearly demonstrated by this grouping of aspects, but we have to suspect the existence of those pesky thorns under all the wonderful roses of success. Jupiter and Uranus together suggest excess. The anti-Communist activity of the McCarthy era was excessive by modern standards. The Watergate break-in was completely outside the law. Nixon paid the price for that mistake—he was forced to resign or face legal battles that could have destroyed both him and the office of the president.

The semisextile aspects in Nixon's birthchart indicate a tremendous desire to expand in several directions. The Sun-Moon semisextile involves both conscious thought and less conscious reaction. Uranus indicates four more directions for expansion:

- Venus—Expansion into a long-term marriage partnership.
- Jupiter—Expansion into reckless optimism that may be larger than life. It also reflects the one-sidedness of Nixon's anti-Communist position. This aspect also reflects his lucky "escape" from the legal entanglements of Watergate via resignation and then a presidential pardon for any illegal acts he "may have" committed during his term of office.
- Mercury—Expansion into a revolutionary spirit, as seen in the decision to go to China and establish a relationship with this powerful and populous nation.

· Mars—Expansion into danger. This aspect is "out of sign" in that Mars and Uranus are not in adjacent signs, as we would normally expect for the semisextile. Traditional astrologers would say this weakens the aspect. In this case, I feel that the close conjunction of Mars to Mercury and Jupiter makes the Mars-Uranus aspect quite strong. That said, the Mars-Uranus semisextile is suggestive of the danger of an overly optimistic view of one's position. While Nixon denied any direct connection to the Watergate break-in, he certainly had encouraged an attitude that his associates should "do whatever it takes" to get him elected.

Richard Nixon's chart is a study in contrasts. On the one hand, he was an effective politician who was responsible for creating a kind of partnership with China. On the other hand, he carried his ideas to the extreme on several occasions, and nearly ruined his political record in the process.

Case Study: Jonas Salk

Because Jonas Salk was not in the limelight as much as Nixon, we don't have an extensive body of information about his private life. However, he is known as the man who created a vaccine against polio, and during his life he also worked to develop vaccines for influenza and AIDS.

His Uranus in Aquarius in the Third House is indicative of his mental capacity. In the same sign as Jupiter, Uranus suggests a desire to expand his knowledge into a new arena and to make revolutionary changes. The conjunction aspect is prominent, with conjunctions of Mercury to Mars and Saturn to Pluto, indicating a strong focus on endings and new beginnings. Neptune is semisextile to both Saturn and Pluto, suggesting that the path to success was not always easy.

By 1952 Salk had tested polio vaccines on monkeys, and in 1954 it was tested on millions of school-age subjects. His work has led to near eradication of this disease, and Albert Bruce Sabin was later able to perfect a live polio vaccine because of Salk's research. The Salk Institute is now working to find a solution to the AIDS problem—a monument to Dr. Salk's dedication to healing.

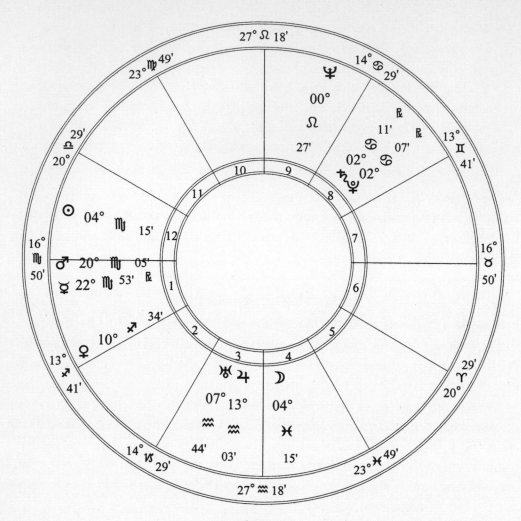

Chart 21

Jonas Salk

October 28, 1914 / New York, NY / 7:30 A.M. EST

Koch Houses

Exercise

Find Uranus in your birthchart.

1. List the aspects to Uranus in your chart.

2. Using your intuition, think about each aspect and how it can help you in the future.

3. Find any semisextiles and quincunxes in your chart. Do they reflect adjustments you have made in the past? How might you work with them now so that future adjustments will be easier?

4. Do some historical research about discoveries that were made around the time you were born.

5. Identify famous people who share your Uranus sign. How did they change themselves or the world?

Summary

Uranus is in each sign for about seven years. While Uranus is in each sign, we are introduced to a new way to develop intuition. As Uranus moves through the signs, it forms new aspects to each planet in our birthchart. Just as the organs of the body are completely renewed every seven years, our extrasensory abilities get a facelift, too. The next chapter looks at Neptune, a planet of psychic sensitivity and of potential illusion.

12
Neptune, the Twelfth House, and the Quintile and Biquintile

In many ways Neptune directly reflects its physical nature in its astrological application. Neptune is much larger than the Earth—49,500 kilometers in diameter compared to 12,750 kilometers—so we could expect big things from Neptune astrologically. Its volume is 57 times that of the Earth, but its mass is only 3.24 times more. We are used to saying, "What you see is what you get," and we mean this in terms of our ordinary experience on Earth. With Neptune, what you see is 57 divided by 3.24, or 17½ times more than what you get. Hence the astrological aphorism that Neptune promises much and delivers little.

Protection or Deception?

How does our aphorism work out astrologically? Neptune is often an indication of where and how we are deceived. We expect a result that never occurs. The illusion of Neptune suggests unrealistic outcomes, based upon unreliable data. Thus we often experience disappointment where Neptune is found, and if not disappointment, then a surreal view of that area of our lives. Neptune is a planet associated with Hollywood and the movies, and with good reason. Acting is all about making us believe in the story we are watching.

Neptune's illusion protects us as well. An obvious example is anesthetics and pain-killing drugs, both of which are associated with Neptune. In this physical example, and in parallel emotional ways, Neptune seems to protect us from realities that would be too hard to bear. The thing to remember is that just because you don't feel the pain, that doesn't mean there isn't a problem. Neptune can mask our problems and prevent us from finding the best way to get through difficulties.

The compassionate values associated with Neptune come from the desire to help others. We know how painful events in our own lives have been, and we want to protect others from experiencing the same problems. The same goes for our friends and for people less fortunate than ourselves. Compassion is a very human response to the needs of others. The best expression of Neptune is reflected in our efforts to help, especially when those efforts spring from wisdom and not from self-delusion. We don't always know what is best for others, and in those cases we can offer sympathy. Sometimes all we can do is share the moment, without needing to take any action. Neptune indicates the way in which we are able to do this, by its sign and house placement.

Neptune, like all the planets, reflects in every plane of experience. Its nature is diverse and wonderful.

Physical

Insidious progress, difficulty in diagnosis. Neptune indicates the hidden side of any physical problem. It has to do with infection, for example. Until rather recently in human history, we didn't even know about germs and viruses. Once we could see them through microscopes, we began to understand the nature of disease better. Still, some illnesses progress unseen and unfelt, until it is too late to heal the problem.

Mental

Imagination. This side of Neptune is reflected in art, movies, music, and other areas of life where our thoughts give rise to new inventions and new expressions of our feelings. We are able to imagine what is not seen and to fantasize about what may happen in the future. In this way we are able to wrap our experiences in new, ever more amazing fabrics.

Emotional

Despair versus fantasy. If we have been deluded, or even if we have only been overprotected, we can feel despair when we realize the extent of our error. We don't generally expect to be led astray so thoroughly. If we are using drugs or alcohol to mask our real pain, whether physical or emotional, we will suffer even more when the drug is no longer available. Neptune indicates where protection can lead to overprotection.

By the same token, we very much enjoy fantasy. We read fiction and watch movies to escape from the real world. We think up stories in our own minds about how other people might act or about our own potential successes. The key thing to remember is this: fantasy is good; deception is not so good. Learning when, how, and where to make the distinction is important.

Spiritual

Compassion. On the spiritual level we sense the invisible energy that flows around us. We experience the feelings of others from time to time, and we are sometimes pleasantly surprised when they sense ours. Some people see auras, foresee future events, and become aware of events occurring in distant places. Most of us never have these experiences, or at least never realize it. I do feel that more people are opening to these experiences, perhaps because we now have mechanical means of seeing distant events unfold and hearing from people who are far away.

Neptune Through the Signs

Throughout this book I have tried to provide concise information about each planet, sign, house, and aspect. Arriving now at Neptune, the most precise thing to be said is that there is nothing definite about its energy. It is realistic to have such an energy identified in astrology, as so much of life is imprecise. Because Neptune moves so slowly, we will not know living persons who have Neptune in every sign. For this reason I have included some historical figures, along with more contemporary people, as examples of the best Neptune has to offer.

Neptune in Aries

This placement indicates a less selfish attitude than might be expected with other planets here. Such a person is sensitive to the environment and to others. People with Neptune here have produced some of the most impressive contrasts in motivation and imagination. They include William Randolph Hearst, Swami Vivekananda, Henri Toulouse-Lautrec, Henry Ford, and Wilbur Wright.

Neptune in Taurus

Neptune in Taurus indicates an individual with exquisite taste and creative design capabilities. There is often a practical sense of position in social situations. Income may come from unusual sources. People with this placement of Neptune include Winston Churchill, Robert Frost, Carl G. Jung, Mata Hari, and Wallace Stevens.

Neptune in Gemini

Neptune here indicates impressionability. It also suggests the capacity to tell a wonderful story, even an inspired one. There may be a desire to engage in mystical activities, as the capacity to communicate across planes of existence is strong. People with Neptune in Gemini include Raymond Chandler, Joseph P. Kennedy, Adolf Hitler, Edna St. Vincent Millay, and Mae West.

Neptune in Cancer

When a watery planet and a water sign combine, the outcome is a profound potential for spiritual understanding. The feeling nature can be tuned to communion with others. There can be suffering if events bring disappointment. Walt Disney had Neptune in Cancer, along with Grant Lewi (a well-known astrologer), Dr. Benjamin Spock, Ayn Rand, Greta Garbo, and Anne Morrow Lindbergh.

Neptune in Leo

Powerful enthusiasm is fueled by imagination with Neptune in Leo. The ability to play a role is complemented by the capacity to project sexuality, making for grand acting. There is a love of all things beautiful. Lena Horne exemplifies the magnetism of this placement, along with Phyllis Diller (what a contrast!), Indira Gandhi, Art Carney, Isaac Asimov, and Charlie Parker.

Neptune in Virgo

Neptune in Virgo indicates the intuition to understand others, and this may come through physical awareness of the feelings of others. You may have healing hands or other healing abilities. There also may be an intense sensitivity that can get in the way of your personal activities. People with this placement include Edward Kennedy, Johnny Cash, Elizabeth Taylor, Beethoven, and Mozart. Other contemporaries include Muhammad Ali, John Lennon, and Jack Nicklaus.

Neptune in Libra

This placement indicates the capacity to understand people beneath their social veneer—and some people with this placement have profound psychic insight. They tend to resonate with people from the previous Neptune generation like Byron, Shelley, Davy Crockett, and Jane Austen. Names like George Harrison, Cher, and Prince Charles grace the list of contemporaries with Neptune in Libra.

Neptune in Scorpio

People with Neptune in Scorpio are deeply committed to the study of metaphysical, and even mediumistic, subjects. They can reach the depths of depression or the heights of imagination. This placement indicates sharpened senses. Notables with this placement include Honoré de Balzac, Ralph Waldo Emerson, Mary Shelley, Tom Cruise, Madonna, and Caroline Kennedy.

Neptune in Sagittarius

Neptune in Sagittarius indicates foresight of an almost magical nature. This also reflects the ability to make plans based on faith. There can be a lack of discrimination in the present. Catherine of Aragon, Abraham Lincoln, Charles Darwin, P. T. Barnum, Charlotte and Emily Brontë, Queen Victoria, Ben Affleck, Kyoko Ina, and Monica Lewinsky share this placement of Neptune.

Neptune in Capricorn

Neptune here suggests the capacity to engage in serious research into scientific, religious, or other subjects. There can also be a sense of nonreality attached to one's life. Meditation practice comes easily. Clara Barton, Louis Pasteur, Leo Tolstoy, Helena Blavatsky,

Osel Hita y Torres (the reincarnation of Lama Thubten Yeshe), and Jon Benet Ramsey share this placement.

Neptune in Aquarius

There is an intense desire for a soul mate. There is also a capacity to change oneself and one's world. There can also be a lack of truthfulness or sincerity, or at the more positive end of the scale, noble goals. People with Neptune in Aquarius include Andrew Carnegie, Mark Twain, J. P. Morgan, Sarah Bernhardt, Jesse James, Saint Teresa of Avila, Saint Bernadette, Annie Besant, and Catherine de Medici.

Neptune in Pisces

Neptune is comfortable in Pisces, its own sign. There is a reserve or calm on the one hand, and the tendency to overuse drugs on the other. This is a good placement for artistic pursuits, as there is a psychic connection to the environment. There can be profound pessimism, too. Elizabeth I of England, William of Orange, Napoleon, Vincent Van Gogh, Sigmund Freud, Annie Oakley, Rudolph Steiner, Edith Wharton, Lizzie Borden, and Emanuel Swedenborg all had Neptune in Pisces.

The Twelfth House

Neptune is associated with the zodiacal sign of Pisces, and Pisces is the sign naturally placed in the Twelfth House. The physical connection to the Twelfth House is through the feet and toes. The feet provide the foundation for physical movement, and they metaphorically are the foundation for understanding ourselves and the world around us.

The Twelfth House has a bad rap in some astrologers' eyes. It is sometimes said to be where you can read your downfall and bad habits, for example. This house does reflect secrets of all kinds and often indicates the nature of your mystical associations. And it is often true that our troubles, as well as our downfall, are caused by secrets. But that doesn't make the Twelfth House bad. There is a constructive side to mysticism and secret matters. Most areas of life have both constructive and less constructive elements.

The Twelfth House is associated with institutions of all kinds, including hospitals, prisons, charitable institutions, and any place of confinement. Planets here function well in private, and they also indicate how we experience confinement and what kind of people we meet in confining situations. If there are no planets here, then confinement occurs as a result of activity elsewhere in the chart. For example, Neptune in the Fifth House of a woman's chart may indicate a hospital stay associated with childbirth.

The planet associated with the sign on the Twelfth House often indicates an area where the individual engages in private activities. For example, if Leo is on the Twelfth-House cusp, as in Tiger Woods' chart, and the Sun is in the Fourth House, then home life will be kept private. For Celine Dion, Cancer is on the Twelfth-House cusp, and the Moon is in the Tenth House. We can say that for her, family is her career in some ways, and that much of her career activity takes place in private.

The Quintile and Biquintile Aspects

The quintile and biquintile aspects are not used by many astrologers, but they provide a unique perspective on talent and creativity. The word quintile has a root meaning of five, and the quintile is derived by dividing the 360 degree circle by five. The quintile is 72 degrees and the biquintile is 144 degrees. Like the semisquare and sesquisquare, this pair of aspects may connect signs of different elements and modes. This depends on what degree the planets occupy in the chart.

The quintile and biquintile reflect creative exchange between planets. They focus on talents and abilities that are fundamental and natural. The quintile indicates talents that express in the exterior world easily. They indicate planetary energies that not only work easily together, but also create measurable outcomes or products. The biquintile indicates how the mind works on a creative problem. The creativity may never manifest in a specific project on the material level. All the action takes place within the individual's own mind.

In order for quintiles and biquintiles to express fully in your life, you have to let go of ego. Think of the small child learning a new task. Recall the exuberance both of the learning process and the mastery. Babies laugh out loud when they accomplish new goals. They are not concerned about how they look to others. They are fully focused on the task at hand, and they experience joy both in the learning and in the doing. We can learn from them.

Case Study: Celine Dion

Celine has no quintiles in her chart, but she has two biquintiles, including a Moon-Pluto biquintile. Recalling the basics about Moon and Pluto, located in Aries and Virgo, we can build an interpretation. The less conscious activity indicated by the Moon in Aries is impulsive, and it seeks personal control. Pluto is about power and will, and in Virgo we see the potential for research into practical solutions for problems. The biquintile suggests that these energies blend on the interior plane. Therefore we can say that Celine is skilled at problem solving, and that she does this within herself. Her actions make the most sense in terms of her inner decision-making process, and may not seem to make sense to others at first glance.

Celine also has a Mars-Uranus biquintile. Mars is in Taurus and Uranus is in Virgo. Mars in Taurus indicates strength and endurance, but it can devolve into stubborn resistance. Uranus is about the rhythm and equilibrium of life, and in Virgo it suggests the use of intuition to maintain the rhythm. This intuition needs practice if it is to be consistent and effective. This biquintile indicates that Celine finds her strength within herself. She intuitively understands what is most important to her, and does not get drawn into believing what her fans or other people say.

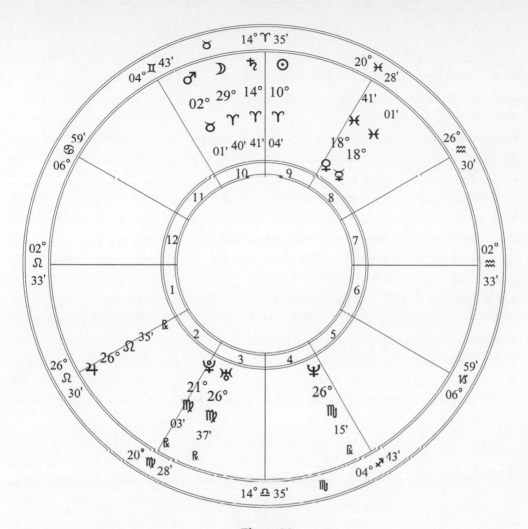

Chart 22
Celine Dion
March 30, 1968 / Charlemagne, Québec / 12:15 P.M. EST
Koch Houses

Case Study: Tiger Woods

Tiger Woods has two quintiles, Moon to Pluto and Saturn to Pluto. He also has two biquintiles, Moon to Saturn and Mercury to Mars. We think of Tiger Woods as being a great golfer. Some of you may not think of golf as a creative activity like the way you think of singing or painting. If we define creativity more broadly, it encompasses all kinds of activities in which we either engage in material work to make things happen, or we engage in the interior world to experience positive personal change. In both senses, we can conclude that Tiger is very creative.

With the Moon and Saturn quintile Pluto, Tiger's less conscious mental process and his approach to the structure of his activities both have a force factor present. He pushes himself to be the best he can be, and he looks to the environment—not just to golf—for his inspiration. His golf game exemplifies the creative touch, particularly when he has made a poor shot and needs to retrieve his playing position on the next one. He has tremendous control of his physical body and uses it as a weapon or tool.

When we add in the Moon biquintile to Saturn, we see that the Moon, Saturn, and Pluto all relate to each other through this family of aspects. When a pattern like this forms, the synergy is heightened. Tiger's talent lies in being able to come at each shot from deep within himself. After the worst shots, he digs down and finds a creative way out of the position, whether it requires lots of power, lots of restraint, or a bit of unconscious instinct.

Finally, Tiger has Mercury biquintile Mars. The inner talent here combines energy and movement. I feel this expresses in at least two ways. First, it expresses internally. Tiger can have a conversation with himself about creative options. Golf, like other things in life, is not about always making good shots. It is about recovering from the missed ones too. It's also about understanding when to press harder and when to relax and enjoy the game. Second, this Mercury-Mars biquintile allows long-term plans to incubate. Tiger knows how to prepare himself for a big tournament. He may do the interior work for days or weeks ahead of time. He also has devised a solid plan for his life outside of golf, establishing a foundation to help kids set and reach goals.

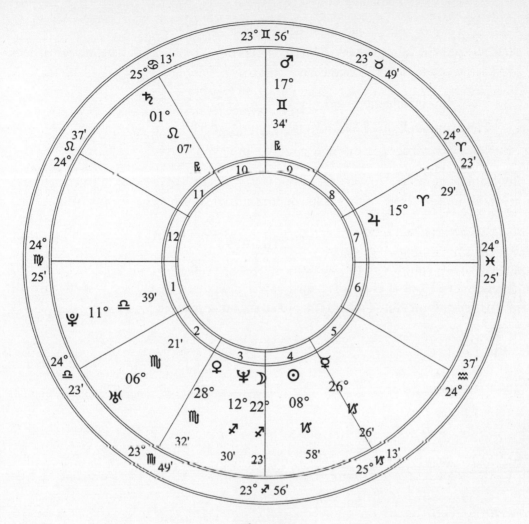

Chart 23

Tiger Woods

December 30, 1975 / Long Beach, CA / 10:50 P.M. PST

Koch Houses

Exercise

Find Neptune in your birthchart. What aspects does it make? Looking at each aspect, what can you say about the following:

- How your imagination works
- How you can be misled or misunderstood
- How you are developing compassion for others

Look at any quintiles. How are they associated with creative projects in your life? Look at any biquintiles. How do they help you understand your internal creative process?

Summary

Neptune is an indicator of imagination, illusion, delusion, and compassion. In the next chapter we will look at Pluto, the planet of will and power. We will see how effective use of will depends on Pluto's relationship to all the other planets.

13
Pluto, the Eighth House, and Synthesis

From its discovery until recent years, Pluto has been considered the outermost object in our solar system, other than comets. It is an unusual planet in many respects. Its orbit is in a very different plane from the ecliptic (the path of the Earth around the Sun). It has a Moon, Charon, that is more like a companion, with a diameter over half that of the planet. Because the orbital speed of Charon and the revolutionary speed of Pluto are the same, Charon has a fixed position over the planet.

The energy of Pluto has two distinct expressions. One is that of the Trickster archetype. Pluto indicates the area of life where we experience profound change—so intense that we say it transforms us. Sometimes the impulse to change is self-evident, as when individuals leave us through death. Other times, though, the change is on an internal, emotional, or spiritual level, and not so obvious.

The second energetic expression of Pluto is that of the Fool. The Fool can be a raw beginner, setting out without much of a clue as to what can be discovered in life. Stepping off the edge of a cliff is a real possibility because cliffs represent the unknown. The Fool can also be a person who has gone around the block a few times, learning lessons with each experience. In this case we are starting out fresh, all right, but we are not un-informed about the possibilities life has to offer. Pluto can signal the beginning of a new episode but does not deny what has been learned in the past.

Like the other planets, Pluto is experienced on all levels of our being. Its power has a creative, almost ecstatic potential, and at the same time there is a dark, terrible side to this energy. Let's look as some of the possibilities.

Physical

Recklessness. The Fool can mindlessly step off the edge of a precipice, heedless of the dangers in the physical environment. Physical destruction also comes through the in-ability to regulate the application of power (force) in a situation, when irresistible force meets the immovable object. Positive transformation occurs when the right amount of force is applied. An example of this is the use of medicines in healing. The proper amount not only leads to the healing of illness or injury, it also encourages the body to strengthen and heal itself.

Mental

Obsession and compulsion. The Fool metaphor works here as well. Irresistible will allows obsessive thought to be carried into compulsive expression. If this energy is expressed in physical work or artistic expression, then the product is positive. On the other hand, if the obsession to control others leads to emotional coercion, the results are destructive to the relationship.

Emotional

Resistance. The power of Pluto can generate resistance within the personality. Resistance is a good thing in its proper measure. Generally, when we place objects on a table, we ex-pect the force of gravity to hold them where we put them. Occasionally we find a lack of resistance. Most of us have experienced slipping on ice or a waxed floor or in a bathtub. The unexpected happens. When we experience mental resistance, we often think of it as an undesirable thing. Resistance can keep us from what we believe we want, yet it also allows us to concentrate on one topic without distraction.

Spiritual

Transcendence. Pluto can transmute our beliefs in an instant or over a long period of awakening. We can be instantly converted, like Saint Paul, or we can gradually come to realize that we are very different from the person we were five or ten years ago. Hyacinths pop out of the ground and bloom very quickly, while a grapevine needs three years of growth before the fruit appears. Both produce little round purple things, proving that speed is not always what is needed.

Aspects to Pluto in the birthchart indicate how this powerful force is likely to express in your life. The transcendent force is present, and generally other energies affect it and not the other way around. This is because the faster-moving planet forms the aspect, and therefore comes to any situation with a message for Pluto. As Pluto moves forward through time, however, the force it represents is felt by other planets in the birthchart. This transformative force cannot be held back. Thus it is important to pay attention to our physical, mental, emotional, and spiritual worlds as we go along. We can act as the joyful Fool, laughing as we enter into new experiences. Then we are not so much reckless as we are exuberant. We are not invulnerable, but we are sturdy in every way.

Case Study: J. P. Morgan, Sr.

If you have a planet conjunct Pluto in your birthchart, then you tend to see power as synonymous with that planet. Power will tend to be defined in terms of the other planet in the conjunction. J. P. Morgan had Pluto conjunct Venus. His use of power flowed into his relationships with his business and marital partners. He transformed the financial world by creating combines, or major corporations. He transformed the railroad system by linking short lines together so everyone could use each other's tracks. He also used his power to try to heal his wife's terminal illness, going well beyond what an ordinary person might do. They even went to Europe and sought healing cures. During that time, and during other travels, J. P. Morgan also collected art works for his impressive collection. He invoked Venusian transformation on all levels.

While J. P. Morgan had no sextiles to Pluto in his birthchart, Pluto did move forward by transit to sextile Uranus when he was twenty-two years old. This was about the time he began his working life and met the man who would be his business ally for most of his life. At the same time, however, the focus was on his own persona, as Uranus was in the First House natally. The opportunity of the sextile was to transform the way he used his intuition in conjunction with his work as a banker. For example, he was able to weather the financial panic of 1857 and come out a winner.

The only square of Pluto in his birthchart was to the Part of Fortune. (This point in any chart is the same distance from the Ascendant as the Moon is from the Sun, and it is thought to impart luck to the individual). While J. P. Morgan thought out all his schemes in great detail, he also had luck on his side. Some people say luck is what we make of it, and Morgan was able to grasp the best opportunities throughout his career. With the Part of Fortune in the Fifth House, we can say his luck depended largely on his creative mind.

Morgan had a trine between Mars and Pluto, and also between the Midheaven and Pluto. Trines appear to be easier to deal with than other aspects, and this is often the feeling with Pluto. However, the unconscious expression of these aspects can be explosive. Mars brought great energy to Morgan's use of power, and it is easy to see how this power, if uncontrolled, could be very destructive. History records his brilliant successes, but there were probably some failures, too. The Midheaven connection reflects his ability to convince others to follow his lead in business matters.

There were no oppositions to Pluto in Morgan's birthchart, but during his life Pluto moved by transit to oppose Saturn in the Ninth House between 1866 and 1869, and later to oppose the Midheaven between 1894 and 1897. The Pluto opposition to Saturn occurred during his honeymoon with his second wife in Europe. At that time she became pregnant with his daughter Louisa. During the period of the 1890s, Morgan was fighting for survival because of antitrust legislation. He eventually organized U.S. Steel, a corporation with assets four times as great as the U.S. federal budget. In the first year, U.S. Steel had earnings equivalent to $750 million (in 1990).

J. P. Morgan had two quincunxes involving Pluto, one from the Moon and one from Saturn. These formed a pattern called a Yod, or Finger of God. Saturn at the Ninth-House cusp indicates the significance of travel in Morgan's business success, and the Moon in the Seventh House indicates the importance of partners, both marital and business. The Finger of God points to Pluto in the Second House of self-worth. Morgan was inspired in his ability to make money, and he was also fortunate in his talent for spending it. He was able to make adjustments during the financial bad times and to "make hay" while the financial Sun shone.

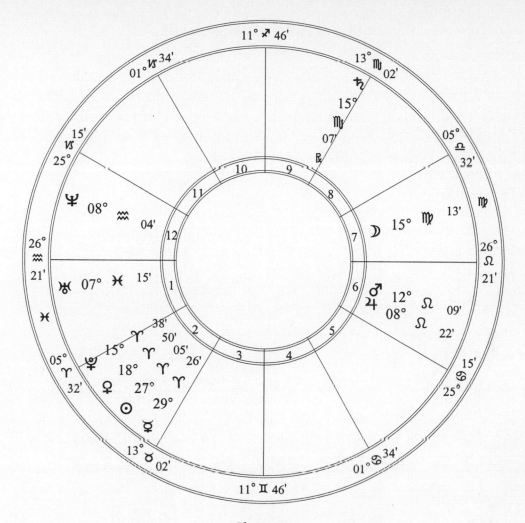

Chart 24

J. P. Morgan, Sr.

April 17, 1837 / Hartford, CT / 3:00 A.M. LMT

Koch Houses

Pluto Through the Signs

Pluto in Aries

The combination of sheer power and deep intuition makes this a powerful placement for Pluto. First, extraordinary energy drives the individual. Second, there is a desire for power. Third, there is a potent intuitive awareness to support both short-term and long-term decision-making. Examples of this placement include J. P. Morgan, Sarah Bernhardt, Thomas Edison, Henry James, and Abdul-Baha.

Pluto in Taurus

Pluto in Taurus is in the sign opposite its own, and therefore not so comfortable. The power of acquisition is strong, but the force applied can be as destructive as an earthquake. Examples of this placement include W. B. Yeats, Sigmund Freud, Arthur Conan Doyle, Swami Vivekananda, Evangeline Adams (an astrologer), Gertrude Stein, and Emily Post.

Pluto in Gemini

Here the power of Pluto is directed into intellectual channels. The result can be powerful speaking ability, deep scientific interest, or the desire to experience new and more exciting adventures. Pluto can lead the individual into strange pursuits, all focused on the transformation of ideas. People with Pluto in Gemini include Sam Goldwyn, Harry Truman, Isak Dinesen, Mark Edmund Jones (a well-known astrologer and originator of the Sabian Symbols), Arnold Toynbee, Georgia O'Keefe, and Mae West.

Pluto in Cancer

Here the influence of family and culture is strong. Pluto in Cancer takes on responsibilities that shape the destiny of society. There can be major breakthroughs in study and research, and there can also be dramatic efforts to accomplish unusual goals. The emphasis on the feeling function indicates that these people are emotionally driven, although this may be largely unconscious. Pluto-in-Cancer people include Anne McCaffrey, Walt Disney, Jonas Salk, Walter Cronkite, John F. Kennedy, Indira Gandhi, Queen Elizabeth II of England, Marilyn Monroe, and Allen Ginsberg.

Pluto in Leo

Strong emotional forces combine with intuition to push these individuals toward some sort of greatness. If Pluto is prominent by house or sign placement and aspect, the individual can emerge from the pack to assume a leadership role. All four of the Beatles have this placement, as do Prince Charles, Tammy Faye Bakker, Karen Silkwood, and Sigourney Weaver.

Pluto in Virgo

The combination of power and discrimination creates the setting for powerful scientific research into practical solutions to problems that plague us all. This generation is capable of accomplishing a lot with what may seem to be limited resources. Once on the "scent," these individuals pursue their goals vigorously. Florence Griffith Joyner is an example of this intense focus, as are Princess Diana, Immanuel Kant, Machiavelli, Michelangelo, and Caroline Kennedy.

Pluto in Libra

There can be great genius with this placement, and it can be used to benefit others or to cause great harm. Because these people have a deep understanding of the balances in nature, they can be major forces for change in any area and may gain celebrity for their works. Examples include Catherine of Aragon, Catherine the Great of Russia, John Adams, George Washington, and Franz Mesmer. It's a bit too soon to predict greatness in the current generation outside the sports and entertainment industries. Some apparent greats include Monica Seles, Ricky Martin, Elvis Stojko, Shaquille O'Neal, and Winona Ryder.

Pluto in Scorpio

Profound unconscious forces surge within the being of these folks. They can be fanatical in their pursuits, beyond all ordinary levels of physical, mental, emotional, and spiritual energy. Pluto is comfortable in this sign, so it functions well, resulting in extraordinary achievement. We can all have high hopes for the Pluto-in-Scorpio generation. Some possible role models include Paracelsus, a great healer and physician; John Hancock, the first to sign the Declaration of Independence; the Marquis de Sade, whose name is immortalized in the term sadism; Antoine Lavoisier, a noted French chemist; and Johannes Charion, a German astrologer and mathematician.

Pluto in Sagittarius

This is a strong placement for the encouragement of advanced knowledge, particularly in spiritual subjects. Intuition concerning the future can be intense, along with philosophical or religious idealism. Travel may be central to success in life. Romulus and Remus, founders of Rome, had this placement. Others include Nostradamus, of prediction fame; Mercator, associated with map-making; Teresa of Avila, a Spanish saint; William Bligh, a British seaman whose crew mutinied; Mozart; and William Blake.

Pluto in Capricorn

This placement indicates a desire, accompanied by serious effort, to be recognized in some way. The combination of Pluto in Capricorn can lead to a dictatorial attitude. It can also lead to remarkable success, probably due to the enormous effort expended. Notable examples of people with this placement are Catherine de Medici, a remarkably cruel Queen of France; Pope Innocent, who had a short reign of only two months; John Dee, British astrologer and spy for Elizabeth I; Ivan the Terrible, who was first pious and then unusually cruel; Thomas Malthus, from whom we got our theories about population; Napoleon; Coleridge; and Jane Austen.

Pluto in Aquarius

Pluto in Aquarius reflects the capacity to make wide-ranging plans and to effect reforms in the social environment. There may be unrealistic hopes that lead to disappointment if not realized. The individual may become popular through sheer force of personality. Mohammed had this placement, as did Omar Khayam; Elizabeth I of England; Beau Brummel, a British dandy; Francis Scott Key; David Brewster, inventor of the kaleidoscope and other optical instruments; and Mary Shelley, creator of Frankenstein.

Pluto in Pisces

With Pluto in Pisces, there is a desire to live in seclusion and to work on the mysteries of the universe. There may be susceptibility to drugs, alcohol, or other addictive temptations. Henri IV of France converted to Catholicism to bring peace to his realm; Sir Philip Sidney embodied the correctness of the gentleman in his era. Other notables include Galileo, who recanted his scientific beliefs; James I of England, who married out of duty; Marie de Medici, who was a disinterested consort but avid regent for her son; and Pope Innocent X, who is said to have been dominated by his sister-in-law. More recent examples include Victor Hugo, Karl Marx, Elizabeth Barrett Browning, Charles Dickens, Mary Todd Lincoln, and George Eliot, who changed her name in order to gain credibility.

The Eighth House

Pluto is the planet closely associated with Scorpio, and Scorpio is naturally found in the Eighth House. The factors that are relevant to the Eighth House include other people's resources, death, rebirth, sexual organs, sexual power, and inheritance. To understand this house, we must somehow understand what these things share in common.

In your own chart, the First House represents you, and the Seventh House is your partner, or more generally other people. The Second House is your personal resources. If you begin with the Seventh House, and think of it as the First House of your partner, then the Eighth House is the Second House of your partner, and therefore your partner's personal resources. You and your partner will inherit from each other if one of you passes on. This is the first connection.

As partners, you share each other's resources in many ways. One of the most significant is the sharing involved in a sexual relationship. Self-esteem grows within intimate relationships when both parties are sharing deeply of their love, commitment, and other resources. Thus the connection with sex is made. The Eighth House reflects the sex organs and creative sexual energy, too. Strong sexual union amplifies creative potential on the one hand, and depletes physical energy on the other.

Ultimately, a profound sexual partnership is part of a greater spiritual partnership. In this kind of connectedness, there is a loss of ego, or what we might call a death of ego. We find ourselves lost in the passion, and indeed no longer separate from the beloved in terms of ego. Complete release of this kind requires surrender. In some marriage ceremonies, the symbolic death of individual egos is a crucial factor. Without giving up one's sense of self to some degree, it is difficult to join fully with one's partner. One way to think of this is that there must be an end to separateness in order to find the beginning of ecstasy.

Another Eighth House factor is surgery. Most surgery is designed to correct a physical problem in order to prolong life or to restore health and mobility. In the act of restoring health, however, there are various small deaths—blood is lost, skin tissue is damaged, organs may be removed. The goal is to heal something within the person, and the cost is loss of some kind.

Thus we find the peaks of physical ecstasy and the pits of dire medical conditions, along with the associated effects on our intimate companions and family members, all tied up in this one house. The capacity for personal transformation is found within the metaphors of the Eighth House. We learn how to make changes in our lives, and we learn how to endure transitions over which we have no control. In the process we learn compassion for ourselves and for others.

Synthesis of the Chart

Bringing all the factors in the chart together into one overall picture of an individual is an intriguing task. Most of the time we look at life one thing at a time. We are not able to encompass all the possibilities in one thought. Yet the chart provides us with all the necessary tools to understand each area of our lives, and to see how those areas are woven together to represent our whole being.

Synthesis means the consideration of all the chart factors that relate to questions we may ask. For example, if we are considering career, we have to look at what the person is capable of doing. Some careers demand great physical strength, others require mental agility, and still others require extensive training. We have to look at all the related factors when we are interpreting the chart.

Still, we tend to do this one thing at a time. This book is organized around one approach to synthesis. We considered one planet, one or two houses, and one or two aspects in each chapter, gradually building a picture of the overall person. By following this pattern through the book, we have seen how each factor is connected to others, forming a net or web of interactivity. Through the case-study charts, we have seen how the same planets, houses, and aspects add up to different expressions of the potential energy we all share.

In looking at the Sun first and then the Moon, we began with the most powerful of the heavenly bodies. All other considerations depend on their position and condition. Then we looked at each of the planets and their associated houses, as well as the significant angular relationships (aspects) among the planets. We also have considered the Ascendant as an indicator of how we present ourselves in the world.

If a particular planet draws your attention, you may want to begin your exploration of the chart with that planet. Consider its placement by sign and house, and then look at the aspects involved. In this way you begin to weave a web with this planet at the starting point, instead of the Sun. For example, if you feel you need more structure in your life, begin with Saturn and see how the various astrological energies are connected to this core concept.

Case Study: Celine Dion

Celine Dion has Pluto in Virgo in the Third House. Pluto is part of a strong opposition pattern: it is conjunct Uranus, and both are opposite Mercury and Venus. In this chapter you read that Pluto in Virgo is capable of research into the nature of a problem. In the Third House, the problem, if you want to call it that, is to communicate. Celine has a marvelous voice, as we would expect from Mercury conjunct Venus. Mercury reflects verbal expression and Venus reflects harmony and beauty. Uranus in Virgo indicates the capacity to move between intuition and practical expression, so we are not surprised to find that Celine reaches deep within herself to create her songs, and then presents them in a convincing manner. She is aware of the effect she has on people, and works to please both herself and her audience with her work.

This one combination in the chart involves four planets. We quickly integrated the energies of the planets, and associated those energies with the conjunctions and oppositions. Now we want to see how this group of planets meshes with the rest of the chart. Since we didn't look at Celine's chart in the Neptune chapter, let's do that now.

Neptune is in Scorpio in the Fourth House, and it shares a sextile with Uranus and Pluto on one side, and a trine with Venus and Mercury on the other. Because Neptune and Pluto move so slowly, everyone born between 1942 and 1999 has these planets sextile to each other in their birthchart. From 1964 to 1969, everyone also had Uranus in a sextile aspect to Neptune and a conjunction aspect to Pluto. This means that all the outer planets were aspecting each other in the charts of everyone born around the same time as Celine Dion. Thus whatever we say about this combination, we will also be saying about all people born between 1964 and 1969.

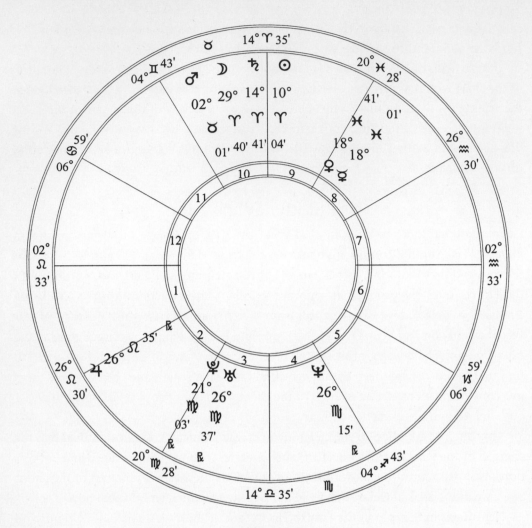

Chart 25

Celine Dion

March 30, 1968 / Charlemagne, Québec / 12:15 P.M. EST

Koch Houses

What can we say definitively about the people in this age group? We can say that they have profound intuition. They are visionaries in terms of education, technology, new forms of communication, computer programming, and advances in every career field. They were born at a time when Americans were sharply divided over the Vietnam War. Their parents may have been hippies.

Neptune is 90 degrees from Jupiter—a square aspect. What pushes Celine to use her intuition is the more philosophical side of her nature. She is probably quite good with money and other Second-House matters. In addition, her self-esteem is highest when she is following her intuitive urges.

Exercise

If you have followed through the book with the exercises, you have considered all the planets, houses, and aspects in your own or someone else's chart. You have seen how each chapter adds a new dimension to your understanding of the chart, and through it, the individual. This exercise is designed to help you gain an overall sense of the chart as a whole.

1. Write one sentence to describe the Sun in the chart. This sentence should be a broad, true, creative statement about the individual.

2. Next write one sentence about the Moon.

3. Now write a few words to describe your impression of how the two work together. To do this you may want to consider the aspect between them, or lack of aspect.

4. Consider the Ascendant and how it expresses the Sun-Moon combination in your personality.

5. Continue this exercise to include all the planets.

6. Finally, write a few words about your impressions of the "story" you have just written. Does the story match up to the way you see and understand yourself or the person whose chart you have used? Pay attention to any areas that are not clear to you. Is there anything in the chart that does not seem to fit at first glance? Perhaps that area is either concealed privately or not yet fully developed. Or perhaps you have discovered a problem that you dealt with in the past and more or less mastered.

7. What have you learned that will help you or the individual whose chart you are interpreting? What creative thoughts arise? Do you have any new insights into your behavior or feelings?

I encourage you to look at any problems you see in the chart, and then set them aside. You may have resolved them in the past and dealt with them, but if not, put them in the past now. Focus on fresh, creative possibilities for your life, earned through your study of this wonderful subject—astrology.

Summary

By this point we have looked at all the points in the chart except for the Midheaven. We have focused on the birthchart, with mentions of the cycles of some of the planets. We have built a picture of the chart, using the many pieces and learning to put them together into meaningful pictures. In the next chapter we will take a brief look at transits—the planetary positions at any point in time. We will see how the charts of two individuals relate to each other, and we will learn how the planets today are related to your birth horoscope to indicate the kinds of events that may occur in your life.

14
Transits

Astrologers have several methods of updating your chart to the present, or to any specific date. While most of them are beyond the scope of this book, we will consider the actual positions of the planets on given dates. These positions are called transits, as the planets are traveling, or transiting, through the zodiac.

Astrological forecasting is done by taking one set of planetary positions and then adding another set to reflect circumstances at a different time. Comparison of the charts of two people does the same thing. If I am born after you, my planets are transits to your chart. I can also compare the charts going the other direction because your planets are simply transits that occurred before I was born.

The rest of this book has focused on one chart—the birthchart. We also looked at the cycles of Saturn and Jupiter and considered events and conditions that might occur during those cycles. Those cycles are made up of transits. Now we want to consider two kinds of charts. First, there are times when you want to know what is happening with your chart right now, or perhaps what was happening at particular time in the past.

Second, you want to compare your chart to someone else's. This kind of comparison is called synastry. You probably won't find this word in your dictionary. The prefix *syn* means "with" or "along with." The last part of the word, *astry*, comes from the root *astr*, which means "star" or "heavens." Comparing the charts of two people means comparing the positions of the planets (stars) on one birth date with the positions on another date. It is the same when we compare current star positions to birth positions. The main difference is that our two people each have a chart that they have lived with for some length of time, and they have become familiar with the energies reflected in those charts. In a way, one person is a "permanent" transit to the other person's chart. Most transits go by rather quickly, and the exact same arrangement won't occur again for a very long time. However, the events and conditions shown by the transits sometimes have long-term effects on our lives.

You have already looked at what the planets mean in the different signs and houses, and what the aspects mean. Now we will see how the moving planet affects the planets in your birthchart. Think of your birthchart as a permanent photograph of the heavens, and think of those planets as being firmly fixed in their positions. The birthchart, as we have seen, is a graphic representation of planetary energies and how they tend to be reflected throughout your life. They are the players who act out their roles in the various rooms on stage (the houses). My rooms are colored somewhat differently from yours by the position of the signs in the houses. In addition, the action in my life drama is different from yours because of the different aspect relationships among the planets.

Think of the transiting planets as new characters playing bit parts. They come into your life drama, do and say what they will, and then move on. Sometimes they do something that affects you for years down the road, and sometimes they simply indicate a telephone conversation or a few thoughts or momentary feelings. The point is that the transits come to visit the birth planets, and not the other way around.

The general rule of thumb, in astrology as on the highway, is that the bigger the planet (truck), the bigger the impact when you make contact. In astrology, bigger means a bigger orbit, or greater distance from the Sun. The exceptions to this rule are the Sun and the Moon, which have tremendous impact on our lives. The Sun is essential to life as we know it, and signals seasonal changes. The Moon is the fastest moving of the heavenly bodies, and its effect is repetitive, but not lasting.

The second part of the rule is this: Because the outer planets are moving much more slowly, we can see or feel them coming. This means that we have time to prepare for them, if we understand astrology. This is the single greatest advantage of astrology—to see what is coming and to prepare for it metaphorically as well as on a practical level.

To examine this rule in greater detail, consider a case in which Pluto today makes an exact square to your Mercury, and at the same time the Moon makes an exact square to your Venus. You can expect a much greater impact from Pluto over a much longer period of time. Just as we allow some orb of influence for aspects in the birthchart, we also allow orbs for transits. In a birthchart we allowed 6 degrees for the square aspect. In the transiting scenario, we only allow 1 degree. This is because we want to focus on a time when the planet will be closest to the aspect. Pluto is within 6 degrees for as much as ten or twelve years. It would be impractical to try to forecast anything specific with this kind of time range.

With a 1 degree orb, Pluto in our example will be in the aspect to Mercury for up to a year and a half, due to the fact that it appears to move forward part of the time, then move backward through the zodiac, and then move forward again. It may not be within 1 degree the entire time, but we tend to continue to feel the effect to some degree. The Moon, by comparison, is within 1 degree of the square for about two hours. We would be busy astrologers indeed if we tried to keep track of every lunar aspect to our chart. How busy? In three days, Celine Dion had nineteen aspects from the Moon, and fifteen aspects from other planets. This means that she had an average of at least eleven potential events during a three-day period.

We need some good ways to sort out all those aspects so we can find the major events. Here are some methods:

1. First, give greater importance to the outer planets. You can figure out the 1 degree orb and usually figure that once the aspect is past, there has to be another aspect to help it along, called a trigger.

2. The triggers are the faster planets, particularly Mars, followed by the Moon. This is because Mars brings energy into the picture, and the Moon brings more energy. If there is no trigger, then a transit may come and go without having much effect.

3. Next, see if the forecast makes sense in the birthchart. The birthchart shows the potential for your life. No event can occur that is not also seen as a potential in the birthchart.

4. Consider also the general environment and circumstances surrounding the individual. For example, even with significant potential in the birthchart and major

transits to indicate it, an Eskimo living in Alaska is unlikely to contract a tropical disease. However, if your Eskimo friend is traveling in Panama, that's a different story.

It may help you to graph the possibilities. If there is an exact Pluto aspect to your Mercury, do a time line showing how long Pluto is within 1 degree. Then graph the time span of other aspects that will occur. See if they involve either Pluto or Mercury. Consider what additional energy these other planets bring to the situation. Are they likely to trigger something?

Three Times Is the Charm

When you are forecasting, you need to have three confirmations of a possible event. The event has to be possible, given the birthchart and the geographical and social factors in the person's life. There has to be a transit indicating the nature of the event. In addition there will be a progression, solar arc direction, or other indication. We won't be considering those in this book, so for our purposes we need to see more than one transit, perhaps one from an outer planet, and one from a faster-moving inner planet.

Case Study: Celine Dion

A lot happened in Celine Dion's life during the years 2000 and 2001.

- She decided to retire temporarily. Her last performance before retirement was on December 31, 1999.
- She became a mom for the first time on January 25, 2001.
- She produced a new album, which was released in March of 2002.
- She developed an entire show for the Las Vegas scene, which began a four to five-year run in March of 2003.

We don't know the exact date on which she decided to retire, but it was not long before her last performance, perhaps weeks. In addition, Celine had some surprise appearances and charity appearances for September 11 victims and for children's charities.

In looking at the time period between her last performance in 1999 and the release of her new album, we find an astonishing lack of aspects from the outer planets. They just aren't hitting her chart the way we would expect for major events in the career of a superstar. Leading up to January 2001, there were some outer-planet transits:

- December 27, 1999—Transiting Neptune leaves its square to Mars in the Tenth House of career in Taurus (voice). The desire for career isn't gone, but it wanes or changes direction after this aspect is complete.

- January 11, 2000—Transiting Neptune completed its opposition to her Ascendant. This planet of ideals and illusions is now in her Seventh House of marriage to stay for a long time. She has made a huge decision about career, marriage, and family. Ideals focus on the significant other/marriage partner. Celine is aware of the depth of her feelings for Rene, and she said she wanted spend more time with him. Neptune moving into the Seventh House shows her obsession and desire shifting more toward relationships and away from work. Celine and Rene reconfirmed their wedding vows on January 2, 2000, with an idealized, exotic ceremony within nine days of the exact aspect.

- June 8 to 17, 2000—Transiting Jupiter opposed Neptune in the Fourth House. Philosophical Jupiter becomes aware of Fourth-House Neptunian ideals concerning family.

- June 6 to July 6, 2000—Transiting Saturn opposed Neptune (Saturn came back again from November 22 to December 19, 2000). The reality of her pregnancy sets in as Saturn structure takes on a new shape, literally. Celine was staying at home a lot during 2001, caring for herself and her pregnancy. Aspects to Neptune in the Fourth House show she has consciously shifted her career focus from singing to motherhood and wife, at least for a while. Transiting Jupiter is in the Tenth House. Jupiter is the planet associated with Sagittarius on the Fifth-House cusp in her chart. With no planets in the Fifth House, Jupiter reveals the creative picture, and that includes both her singing and motherhood. The pregnancy was announced on June 9, 2000. This occurred just as Jupiter entered the opposition to Neptune in the Fourth House. Jupiter was also squaring natal Jupiter *that day*.

Transits from inner planets (not enumerated here) are entirely consistent with this private, personal interlude in Celine's life.

Exercise

Using the ephemeris page included here, compare the positions of the planets on January 1, 2001, to the planets in your birthchart.

1. Are there any outer planets within 1 degree of an aspect to your birthchart?

2. Now look for inner planets.

3. When you find planets within 1 degree of your birth planets, make a list of the transiting planet, the birth planet, and the aspect between them. Write one sentence about each aspect you find that suggests what kind of event may occur.

4. Based on all the aspects, what was that first day of the new millennium like for you? Do the aspects or lack of them reflect how you feel about the twenty-first century?

To determine the transits for any date, simply create a chart using the *Mapping Your Birthchart* CD-ROM for the date you desire. Because the Moon moves so fast (between 11 and 14 degrees each day), you may want to choose a specific time of day.

Summary

This basic introduction to transits shows you the power of astrology in a different way. Once you understand the birthchart, you can carry it forward in time to discover how the potential unfolds and what the new possibilities are for events and conditions. The next chapter wraps up this book with a discussion of the Midheaven.

January 1, 2001 00:00 A.M. EST

Date	☽ Geo Lon	☉ Geo Lon	☿ Geo Lon	♀ Geo Lon	♂ Geo Lon	♃ Geo Lon	♄ Geo Lon	♅ Geo Lon	♆ Geo Lon	♇ Geo Lon
01 01	21°♓13'	10°♑51'	14°♑37'	27°♒12'	05°♏04'	02°♊10'℞	24°♉35'℞	18°♒40'	05°♒20'	13°♐46'
01 02	03°♈28'	11°♑52'	16°♑14'	28°♒18'	05°♏39'	02°♊06'℞	24°♉32'℞	18°♒43'	05°♒22'	13°♐49'
01 03	16°♈01'	12°♑53'	17°♑52'	29°♒24'	06°♏14'	02°♊01'℞	24°♉30'℞	18°♒45'	05°♒24'	13°♐51'
01 04	28°♈56'	13°♑54'	19°♑30'	00°♓29'	06°♏49'	01°♊57'℞	24°♉28'℞	18°♒48'	05°♒26'	13°♐53'
01 05	12°♉16'	14°♑55'	21°♑09'	01°♓35'	07°♏23'	01°♊53'℞	24°♉25'℞	18°♒51'	05°♒29'	13°♐55'
01 06	26°♉03'	15°♑56'	22°♑47'	02°♓40'	07°♏58'	01°♊49'℞	24°♉23'℞	18°♒55'	05°♒31'	13°♐57'
01 07	10°♊17'	16°♑58'	24°♑26'	03°♓45'	08°♏33'	01°♊45'℞	24°♉21'℞	18°♒58'	05°♒33'	13°♐59'
01 08	24°♊57'	17°♑59'	26°♑06'	04°♓49'	09°♏08'	01°♊41'℞	24°♉19'℞	19°♒01'	05°♒35'	14°♐01'
01 09	09°♋55'	19°♑00'	27°♑45'	05°♓53'	09°♏42'	01°♊38'℞	24°♉18'℞	19°♒04'	05°♒37'	14°♐03'
01 10	25°♋06'	20°♑01'	29°♑25'	06°♓57'	10°♏17'	01°♊35'℞	24°♉16'℞	19°♒07'	05°♒40'	14°♐05'
01 11	10°♌18'	21°♑02'	01°♒05'	08°♓01'	10°♏52'	01°♊32'℞	24°♉14'℞	19°♒10'	05°♒42'	14°♐07'
01 12	25°♌23'	22°♑03'	02°♒45'	09°♓04'	11°♏26'	01°♊29'℞	24°♉13'℞	19°♒13'	05°♒44'	14°♐09'
01 13	10°♍12'	23°♑04'	04°♒24'	10°♓07'	12°♏01'	01°♊27'℞	24°♉11'℞	19°♒16'	05°♒46'	14°♐11'
01 14	24°♍38'	24°♑05'	06°♒04'	11°♓09'	12°♏35'	01°♊24'℞	24°♉10'℞	19°♒20'	05°♒48'	14°♐13'
01 15	08°♎39'	25°♑07'	07°♒43'	12°♓11'	13°♏09'	01°♊22'℞	24°♉09'℞	19°♒23'	05°♒51'	14°♐15'
01 16	22°♎15'	26°♑08'	09°♒22'	13°♓13'	13°♏43'	01°♊20'℞	24°♉08'℞	19°♒26'	05°♒53'	14°♐16'
01 17	05°♏25'	27°♑09'	11°♒01'	14°♓14'	14°♏18'	01°♊18'℞	24°♉07'℞	19°♒29'	05°♒55'	14°♐18'
01 18	18°♏13'	28°♑10'	12°♒38'	15°♓15'	14°♏52'	01°♊17'℞	24°♉06'℞	19°♒33'	05°♒57'	14°♐20'
01 19	00°♐43'	29°♑11'	14°♒15'	16°♓16'	15°♏26'	01°♊15'℞	24°♉05'℞	19°♒36'	06°♒00'	14°♐22'
01 20	12°♐58'	00°♒12'	15°♒50'	17°♓16'	16°♏00'	01°♊14'℞	24°♉05'℞	19°♒39'	06°♒02'	14°♐24'
01 21	25°♐02'	01°♒13'	17°♒23'	18°♓15'	16°♏34'	01°♊13'℞	24°♉04'℞	19°♒43'	06°♒04'	14°♐25'
01 22	06°♑58'	02°♒14'	18°♒54'	19°♓15'	17°♏07'	01°♊12'℞	24°♉04'℞	19°♒46'	06°♒07'	14°♐27'
01 23	18°♑49'	03°♒15'	20°♒22'	20°♓13'	17°♏41'	01°♊12'℞	24°♉04'℞	19°♒49'	06°♒09'	14°♐29'
01 24	00°♒37'	04°♒16'	21°♒48'	21°♓12'	18°♏15'	01°♊11'℞	24°♉04'℞	19°♒53'	06°♒11'	14°♐30'
01 25	12°♒25'	05°♒17'	23°♒10'	22°♓09'	18°♏48'	01°♊11'℞	24°♉04'	19°♒56'	06°♒13'	14°♐32'
01 26	24°♒14'	06°♒18'	24°♒27'	23°♓06'	19°♏22'	01°♊11'	24°♉04'	20°♒00'	06°♒16'	14°♐34'
01 27	06°♓07'	07°♒19'	25°♒39'	24°♓03'	19°♏55'	01°♊12'	24°♉04'	20°♒03'	06°♒18'	14°♐35'
01 28	18°♓06'	08°♒20'	26°♒46'	24°♓59'	20°♏29'	01°♊12'	24°♉04'	20°♒06'	06°♒20'	14°♐37'
01 29	00°♈13'	09°♒21'	27°♒46'	25°♓54'	21°♏02'	01°♊13'	24°♉05'	20°♒10'	06°♒23'	14°♐38'
01 30	12°♈30'	10°♒22'	28°♒38'	26°♓49'	21°♏35'	01°♊14'	24°♉05'	20°♒13'	06°♒25'	14°♐40'
01 31	25°♈02'	11°♒23'	29°♒22'	27°♓43'	22°♏08'	01°♊15'	24°♉06'	20°♒17'	06°♒27'	14°♐41'
02 01	07°♉52'	12°♒24'	29°♒57'	28°♓36'	22°♏41'	01°♊16'	24°♉07'	20°♒20'	06°♒29'	14°♐43'

Chart 26.

Ephemeris Page for January 1, 2001

15
The Midheaven and Self-Awareness

If you were calculating your birthchart by hand, the first thing you would do is determine the position of the Midheaven. This chapter is at the end of the book because we come back around to the Midheaven in the end to gain self-awareness. Generally, this kind of understanding comes after we have had other experiences related to each of the planets.

The Midheaven is the point in the zodiac that is highest in the sky at the time of birth. Even though it is the most public point in the chart, it is often one of the least understood. We tend to misunderstand ourselves for several reasons: we are taught to be and act a certain way by our families, teachers, and peers; we think of ourselves in terms of our own inconsistent motives; and we are not mature enough to sort out our own realities from those of family, work place, and culture. As we develop, we come to understand ourselves largely through our experiences.

Earlier in the book we found that the Ascendant is not the same as the Sun. The same is true here—the Midheaven is not the same as the Sun. We come into this life very much acting the role of the Sun, and we carry that role throughout our experiences. The

Sun is what we *are*—our individuality. The Midheaven reflects what we know about ourselves, and what we can learn about ourselves. Because it is a public point, it happens that other people may know us better than we know ourselves. Eventually we achieve self-understanding through this very significant point.

Self-Awareness

Self-awareness develops in two ways. The first is through ego consciousness—as we experience life, we relate our external experience to our inner experience. One theory is that we do this through the ego complex. The ego complex is a psychological mechanism that can be thought of as a craft floating on the surface of a lake. Above the surface is all exterior, objective experience, and below the surface is all interior, subjective experience.

Because the Midheaven is the point that reflects ego-consciousness, it is a psychologically sensitive point. We can be emotionally bruised through this point. Other people may not intend to hurt us, but they can be very edgy in their criticisms, and they tend to criticize based on how they understand us. Since the Midheaven is the most public point, it is the most easily attacked. Think about the people you know. Each of them has sensitive "buttons" that you can push to tease them or to attack them. I have found that the most sensitive buttons relate to the Midheaven. In the section about each sign on the Midheaven that follows, I have started with a key phrase about the sign itself. The easiest line of attack is to say that the person "is not" or "can not," related to this key phrase. The simplest way to build confidence is to praise them in this way.

The second way we gain self-understanding is by discovering the inner source. Just as the ego complex mediates between the exterior world and your inner world, it also mediates between what you are aware of in yourself and what is subconscious or unconscious. Sometimes we think of the subconscious as a place filled with all our dreadful thoughts and feelings—things we would rather not see or experience. A broader definition of the unconscious suggests that it is a place filled with whatever we have stored in memory, forgotten, repressed, or never known.

Carl Jung studied human development, and individuation is the name he gave to the lifelong developmental processes we all experience. Individuation, he said, is "bringing to fulfillment the collective as well as the personal qualities of the person."[1] The collective, according to Jung, is a body of knowledge that we inherit from the past and access through the unconscious mind. Relative to the personal unconscious, which contains memories and repressed or suppressed feelings, the collective unconscious is vast and can be a tremendous source of inspiration.

As we begin to tap into the collective unconscious, the inner source provides inspiration and information we need in order to grow into our individualized selves. In the process we usually have to look at some of the experiences and feelings we have buried. The collective pool of experience offers support through this process, and also offers the glorious inspiration that carries us beyond our personal limits into greater self-understanding.

The Midheaven Through the Signs

The Midheaven is part of a polarity that includes the opposite point, called the *Imum Coeli* (IC). In most of the astrological charts you will use, the IC is the cusp of the Fourth House and is opposite the Midheaven, the cusp of the Tenth House. Thinking back to what we learned in chapter 3, one of the basic concepts about the Fourth House is core beliefs. We learn some beliefs from our families and culture. We also develop personal beliefs that resonate with our own souls. These may be significantly different from what we learn from our families, but are nonetheless part of our core beliefs. These are learned or remembered through life experience.

Combine this idea with what you have just read about the ego complex. Each of us has a mental mechanism we use to gather information. If we are open to the larger collective source, we enrich our pool of knowledge. No longer limited to personal experience, we can tap into the collective experience. In the process we come closer to understanding our deepest personal connections to the universe, sorting them out from what we have been taught. We often find that what we have learned through personal experience meshes pretty well with some of our deepest beliefs.

Midheaven in Aries—I know what I am

This key idea exemplifies the sign of Aries at the Midheaven. While the Sun sign Aries is ambitious, the Aries Midheaven is very conscious of ambition as a personal drive. The same is true of the natural optimism, leadership potential, rashness, and even resistance inherent in the Aries way of approaching the world. Out of this particular kind of self-awareness, the Aries Midheaven can respond to the world directly and effectively. You are able to develop plans of action and follow through with them. Before self-awareness has developed, the Aries Midheaven was more reactive, falling into patterns learned in childhood. As ego-consciousness develops, you are better at responding to outside stimuli and discriminating between major problems and temporary irritations.

Let's look at the capacity for discriminating awareness. This ability is shared by the fire signs on the Midheaven, each expressing it in a unique way. For Aries there is an ability to seek and maintain an intimate relationship, and this ability grows out of the awareness of what you are, deep within yourself. If you understand yourself, then you are able to commit fully to an individual who you perceive will share and honor you for what you are, not for what he or she wants you to be. The less conscious capacity for compassion has been cultivated and brought into consciousness.

The Aries Midheaven learns to make conscious choices. While it may seem that we all learn to do this, for Aries it is a matter of bringing the choice-making mechanism fully into consciousness. Instead of making snap decisions and later wondering why you chose that way, you learn to consider the choices first. Even when you are certain what you will do, you can think through the possibilities and identify why you are discarding others in favor of the one you finally act upon. The Aries impulse is to not waste even a moment on the decision. The self-aware Aries Midheaven knows that one minute spent considering a decision can save time down the road.

Midheaven in Taurus—I know what I have

For starters, this means knowing your own strength. Taurus can push through huge obstacles, but the physical and emotional price can be very high. The Taurus Midheaven understands the concept of personal limits. You know how to preserve your strength. You no longer exhaust all your energy in one effort. Instead you apply a practical amount of energy, and if you don't get you the results you want, you move on to something else. At the same time you have the persistence needed to complete big projects. You learn how to stay on task and avoid wasted trips down side roads.

Security is a Taurus issue. The Taurus Midheaven knows appropriate security boundaries. You know what kinds of situations to avoid completely—they are the ones that are seemingly innocuous, but that lead to deep feelings of insecurity. You also recognize the situations that many people fear, but which you are able to push through to success. An adjunct to handling security issues is the development of tolerance and trust. You learn how to identify those people and situations you can trust. It is as though you see all the sand on the beach and immediately know where the quicksand is. Then, if you decide to go there, you take a rope along and tie it securely to a tree, so you can pull yourself out after you have grabbed the prize you see there.

The less conscious Taurus can have a stingy side or can demonstrate fierce territoriality. This often comes from an unconscious desire to fill a void that was experienced in childhood, or possibly in a past lifetime. The Taurus Midheaven learns to modify this tendency and to complement it with a more sharing attitude. Then you discover one of the rules of the universe: the more you share, the more you get. You always have enough. The basis for greater openness is the ability to explore the territory without judging its value. You learn to take the time to explore before you make irrevocable decisions.

The Taurus Midheaven has a profound understanding of the entire growth cycle. Wherever you find yourself in the process of birth, death, and rebirth, you understand the value of each moment. You see your own life against a background of larger cycles of the planets and of the universe, and you are therefore able to avoid getting stuck in one moment of apparent need. This greater self-awareness provides the mechanism for living simply and enjoying each day. You are able to let go of those things you no longer need without feeling as though you have lost something. In fact, you enjoy having open space around you, so that you can enjoy the things you have. Spaciousness is equated with comfort.

Midheaven in Gemini—I know what I think

Gemini is a thinking sign. The energy can fly all over, like a butterfly moving from flower to flower, soaking up a bit of whatever is available. Beneath this seemingly aimless wandering, the Gemini Midheaven is accumulating essential information for future action. Yes, there is extraneous mental activity, but by engaging in it, you define the more important ground for your active lifestyle.

Moving from flower to flower is fun. However, it also instills a particular view of life's impermanence. There is the sense, on one hand, that there will always be another flower. Beneath this there is a sense that some flowers, if treated well, can last far longer. An example of this is relationships. You can miss the truly important ones if you are moving from one to the next too fast. Perhaps you need to observe the diversity in order to appreciate the one relationship that matters most.

Effective action depends on both perceiving the broader picture and taking effective action in the moment. You learn to pace your activities so that you can move quickly when that is needed, or move not at all when stillness is required. You require enough time and space to make your best decisions. How much is enough? The amount you need. You learn not to be pressured to decide before you are comfortable with your choices. When you only have unpleasant choices, this is even more important. As you develop your sense of space, you find you can make decisions instantly when you have to, and you can feel good about them. By cultivating your thought process, you develop even greater flexibility of choice.

Midheaven in Cancer—I know what I feel

When on the Midheaven, the emotional sensitivity of Cancer is strengthened by awareness of itself. You are able to perceive energy flowing around you and understand it without "being" it. You don't have to sink in the feelings. Instead you are able to bump up against them and remain objective. You retain your sense of self in the midst of emotional turmoil.

With Cancer at the Midheaven, you are capable of a wide range of emotional responses. The scale of possibilities between raging anger and placid calm is filled with almost infinite variety. Through difficult experience you have almost mastered self-control. Once in a while you have to weather an emotional storm. Through this process you develop sympathy for other people who have less control. And you trust that your emotional outburst, how ever huge it seems, is merely one drop in the ocean of feeling.

Depending on your level of mastery, you find that a steady flow of emotional energy fuels your creativity. Rushes of energy sweep you along in their undertow, while a steady stream of energy moves all your projects forward and avoids obstacles by flowing around them. You also allow your conscious thoughts to seep into your inner being, where they energize less conscious mental activity. Later they reemerge in a steady fountain of inspiration.

Midheaven in Leo—I know my own will

Leo Midheavens consciously set high goals for themselves. You temper your ideas and your ideals in the fire of creativity, and you rely on intuition as a source of inspiration. You know that if you are patient, ideas will come to you.

If you believe you are better than other people, you are in for some harsh surprises. You know and understand your own capabilities, and you need to understand that everyone has their own strengths. You only set yourself up for eventual failure if you feel you are perfect. You are well advised to be generous with your support and praise. In this way you raise others to your level instead of separating yourself from them.

Because you don't settle for less than your best, you are a powerful leader. You know how to motivate others because you are able to motivate yourself. You understand your ability to organize. You can be a neighborhood activist or a corporate executive, as you understand group dynamics. You are a humorous person. Underneath your capacity to entertain, you are very sensitive to the nuances of humor. You don't like to be the target of other people's jokes, and this provides you with the capacity to be funny without doing it at someone else's expense. You thus maintain your own dignity and support other people in theirs.

Midheaven in Virgo—I know that I analyze

The Virgo Midheaven serves others consciously. This means there are very few unintentional blunders in your work with other people. You pay attention to nuances of personality and feeling that others would miss. Your life of service is powered by your profound empathy. Your ability to respond to the needs of others is supported by your ability to find the middle ground in any argument. You manifest the possibility of agreement through your exploration of the differences between the parties.

You are very comfortable in the midst of the details of any situation. In fact, when nothing much is happening you may worry that nothing will happen. Empty space, for you, was meant to be filled. The key to conscious living is to fill that space with something worthwhile. One way you do this is to reach into your deepest inner resources. There you find empathy and the capacity for psychic awareness. On the psychic level you will never find complete emptiness.

You consciously use your analytical skills in your daily life. You communicate clearly about the basic demands of any situation, and you are able to line up the facts in an orderly progression from your starting point all the way through to the end result. Along the way you align your goals with the needs of others.

Midheaven in Libra—I know how I balance

Libra stands poised in the middle ground, experiencing the extremes on both sides, but striving to remain in the point of equilibrium. The Libra Midheaven becomes fully aware of the precariousness of this balance. Like a tightrope walker, the Libra Midheaven is at greatest risk when there is no movement. Balance is all about the subtle shifting of weight, on the mental as well as the physical plane. You know how to maintain this balance. Because you are skilled at moving with the energy around you, you rarely need to respond to strength with equal strength. An adaptive response is almost always better.

Your desire for equilibrium is occasionally put to the test. Sometimes you must engage in battle in order to achieve your desired goals. When this happens, you are fully capable of taking extreme measures. All the while, you are designing your strategy to bring you back to harmony. When others recommend drastic attack, you regroup, gather your forces, and plan an orderly assault on the problem. In the long run, this economy of energy works in your favor.

Effective action, for you, depends on the ability to maintain your own balance and to make use of the energies around you. If you become overconfident, you can be fooled by circumstances. You fail to see the subtleties because you are focused on the big picture. Your power lies in your capacity to accommodate the needs and desires of others while maintaining an objective appreciation of what other people can accomplish. Your sense of balance teaches you to nudge, not shove.

Midheaven in Scorpio—I know my own desires

The Scorpio Midheaven is ambitious. You never fool yourself into thinking there is any other reason for your actions. If you are conscious—and you have probably worked hard to become conscious—you know exactly where your desires are leading all the time. If, on the other hand, you believe you are all-knowing and all-powerful, you will face severe tests again and again, and eventually you will fail. The key here is to know your strengths, know your limitations, and know how to turn apparent limitations to your advantage. In this way your desires are fulfilled with a minimum expenditure of emotional energy.

Your inner resources include the ability to be practical. This may seem like a strange statement, as you know your skills. However, practical decisions often demand that you take a more reserved role, so that other forces can come into play. You can reach into the very earth for energy, and you can establish your position solidly without expecting any particular response from others. When you do this, you reserve your own energy and allow others to engage in dialogue with you.

Your profound awareness of the rhythms of life and death has positioned you to take chances when the moment is right. You can walk right up to the edge of a problem, look down into the abyss, and not recoil in fear. Instead you gather understanding of the nature of the precipice so that in the future you don't have to get that close to the edge again.

Midheaven in Sagittarius—I know my own aspirations

Your capacity to plan, whether it is in your career, private life, or interpersonal relationships, depends on the innate intuition of Sagittarius. At the Midheaven, Sagittarius knows the importance of intuition. However, intuition is not a skill most of us can call upon at will. You have to cultivate it and learn how it flows. You have to develop an appropriate channel. You eventually find that it is a lot like a telephone call, with a very clear connection. This takes some effort, though.

Your open-minded approach to life takes you into a wide variety of experiences. You welcome an adventure and know that your philosophical side benefits from new experiences. Your self-awareness allows you to consider many different ideas and philosophies without endangering your personal belief system. Thus the adventure is a lot of fun, it keeps you vitally involved in life, and it tests your intuition by challenging you to prepare for whatever may come.

You sometimes feel terribly lonely. This occurs when you plumb profound spiritual or philosophical depths and discover that no one has accompanied you on this mental journey. Oddly enough, you become a consumer to protect yourself from the pain. You try something, enjoy it, and then discard it. You continually seek something new. You resolve this spending cycle by engaging with the people around you instead of only engaging with ideas. As you develop relationships, you find that new ideas arise. Even though you go off on mental tangents every so often, you benefit from this compassionate exchange of energy.

Midheaven in Capricorn—I know skillful means

Most of the time the Capricorn Midheaven is self-confident and knows it. You are like the mountain goat that can climb the steepest slopes, and then get back down safely. You are surefooted in your approach, especially where career is concerned, but also in social situations. You gravitate toward situations that are practical, stable, and secure.

You are able to concentrate on your work better than most people. You know how to formulate a plan so that you accomplish tasks in an orderly way. Again like the goat, you set a high goal, and then you map out a strategy for achieving it. You don't go all the way out in left field unless that is where you want to end up. You know you are capable, so a new task is exciting, not daunting. People like to work with you because you are dependable. They may not be your best buddies, but they like the secure feeling that you will produce results, on time and close to budget.

Even when you are very successful, you maintain rather simple tastes. You understand that people will measure your success by how you dress, where you live, and how you enjoy life. And you do enjoy life. However, you were also happy living in a two-bedroom apartment when you started out, and you could do that again if need be. Your self-awareness is durable, even in a crisis. You are likely to make a dent in history with your work.

Midheaven in Aquarius—I know that I know

The Aquarius Midheaven gathers all sorts of information, with the ultimate goal of achieving self-understanding. The goal is admirable, but the information collected in the process may include a lot of irrelevant, or even meaningless, information. Thus the Aquarius Midheaven learns through experience to sift out the meaningful facts before filing them in easily accessible memory files. You may anticipate outcomes, but will benefit yourself and others by allowing the process to unfold by itself.

Knowing what you know is only part of the picture for the Aquarius Midheaven. You also need to develop the fine art of choosing the right time to apply your knowledge. Your management skills develop as you learn the refinements of timing. You also need to develop good intervention skills. Even when used at the right moment, a sledgehammer approach lacks subtlety.

The Aquarius Midheaven has the capacity to understand the dimension of space as well as time. This comprehensive view allows you to balance a variety of activities. Sometimes, though, you get lost in the overview and lose track of the details, or vice versa. In either case, you can draw upon your intuition. It's as if you have a little gyroscope that steers you toward the information you need.

As you gain experience, you develop your mind. You find that logical use of intellect, when paired with intuition, provides better answers to life's questions. Each successful decision becomes part of the platform from which you make the next decision. Knowing becomes an integral part of your life, until you "know" on the spiritual level, too. Knowing with such certainty provides the strength you need.

Midheaven in Pisces—I know what I believe

The Pisces Midheaven does not jump into life. You are more likely to take your time developing a sense of self that is adaptable and instinctual. You recognize the instability or impermanence of life, and you therefore don't count on things remaining the same for very long. You know that you are impressionable, so you take in an experience, sit back, and wait to see how it unfolds for you. Through this process you develop strong compassion for the people around you who do jump right in, and find themselves in deep water.

You appreciate the simple things in life. You prefer elegance to flashiness. You may tend to wear monochromatic clothing, for example, but that clothing is not cheap. It fits beautifully and suits your personality. Your decorating style may be extra spacious and elegantly simple. Simplicity extends into your career. You can be kept busy pursuing one thing in life.

You are not willing to make constant changes in your life. You enjoy a routine, and may become attached to it. Even minor changes are upsetting. You learn that you can rearrange your schedule to accommodate other people, but you also learn not to offer to do so. There has to be a very good reason before you adapt, and you probably expect reciprocation.

As you develop self-awareness, you learn that you have held on to old pain in some cases. Letting go is hard because you are uncomfortable with the empty space you believe will exist when the pain is gone. This fear is more urgent than your desire to stop hurting. Since you also feel the pain of others, and their joy, you develop the capacity to feel in the moment, and then go on to the next moment with the expectation that it will be filled with its own emotional energy. Openness to this flow of energy is not easy to develop, but it makes your life a lot more interesting.

Exercise

As a final exercise, let's bring together everything you have learned about the planets, signs, houses, and aspects. We will combine that with what you know about yourself, through understanding your Midheaven. In this way you can see the role free will plays in shaping your personality and your life in general.

1. Review what you have learned about your Sun and Moon signs. How do they work together to reflect your actions in the world and your inner thoughts?

2. Add to this pair the Ascendant. Recall what you discovered about how the Sun, Moon, and Ascendant come together to indicate your personality.

3. Now think about each of the planets and their aspects. How do they indicate the way you use their energies in your daily life? In your relationships? In your career or study interests? What outcomes are suggested by each combination of energies?

4. Consider the sign on your Midheaven. What does it tell you about yourself? What does it indicate that you have yet to learn about yourself?

5. Now look at the aspects that involve the Midheaven. These are indications of the kinds of experiences you encounter that open you to greater self-understanding. Do these aspects indicate constructive experiences? Not so constructive?

6. How does self-awareness impact your life, indicated by the houses where you find the planets that aspect the Midheaven?

Finally, try to summarize all this information into one or two sentences that capture the essence of who you really are. Are these sentences in any way a surprise to you? In some ways they will resonate deep within your heart as they connect to your life force. You will see how they reflect what has always been true and what will continue to be important in your life. The little surprises you have discovered are indications that astrology has served its purpose in revealing something refreshing about the "real" you.

The astrology you have learned in this book can be applied to yourself, to your family and friends, and even to events that occur around you. The CD-ROM allows you to create charts for yourself, family, and friends, and it also provides you with a tool to quickly gather information about the planets and the signs they occupy in a chart. While it is not intended to provide everything you would get in a professional astrology consultation, it does summarize some of the main points about the astrological chart.

The key to astrology is to first understand the person or thing whose chart you are studying. You have to grasp who the person is and what the background may be. You have a unique relationship to each of the planets because of their arrangement in your birthchart, and this is true for each individual. Each person will learn about himself or herself through unique personal experiences that are reflected in the birthchart. It is through the combination of knowing the individual and knowing the birthchart that you become skilled in the use of astrology.

---

1. E. A. Bennet, *What Jung Really Said* (New York: Schocken Books, 1967) 171.

Glossary

Ascendant (rising sign)—The degree and sign of the zodiac that was visible at the eastern horizon at the time of birth. The cusp of the First House. The Ascendant reflects the individual's personality and physical characteristics.

Aspects—Relationships between points in the chart. They are angles measured from the center of the chart. Specific angles are found to be significant:

> **Conjunction (0 degrees)**—Planets that are together in the zodiac. Indicates prominence of the two energies.

> **Semisextile (30 degrees)**—Planets that are exactly one sign apart on the zodiac. Indicates growth; can be uncomfortable.

> **Semisquare (45 degrees)**—Planets exactly one and one-half signs apart in the zodiac indicate internal tension and stress.

> **Sextile (60 degrees)**—Planets that are two signs apart are able to cooperate to produce opportunities.

> **Quintile (72 degrees)**—Planets separated by one-fifth of the zodiac contribute creatively to each other.

Square (90 degrees)—Planets three signs apart indicate challenges.

Trine (120 degrees)—Planets four signs apart indicate comfortable conditions where their energies are concerned.

Sesquisquare, or sesquiquadrate (135 degrees)—Planets four and one-half signs apart indicate agitation, which may not be evident to observers.

Biquintile (144 degrees)—Planets separate by two-fifths of the zodiac indicate the quality of inborn talents.

Quincunx, or inconjunct (150 degrees)—Planets five signs apart indicate the nature of adjustments the individual will be required to make.

Opposition (180 degrees)—Planets opposite each other in the zodiac indicate where the individual will be aware of differences.

Detriment—The sign opposite the sign of rulership. This is a sign where the planet's energy requires effort in order to be successful.

Dignity—A classical astrology term used to indicate comfort or standing of a planet in a particular sign.

Elements—Four designations of principal characteristics of all matter and life.

Fire signs—Energetic, active, impulsive. The fire signs are Aries, Leo, and Sagittarius.

Earth signs—Practical, dependable, conservative. The earth signs are Taurus, Virgo, and Capricorn.

Air signs—Mental, versatile, detached. The airs signs are Gemini, Libra, and Aquarius.

Water signs—Emotional, imaginative, impressionable. The water signs are Cancer, Scorpio, and Pisces.

Exaltation—A classical astrology term for the sign or house where a planet is capable of its best expression, with the possible exception of domicile (the house or sign the planet rules).

Fall—The sign opposite the sign of exaltation. This is a sign where the planet's energy tends to "fall away" from the highest or best expression.

Karma—Conditions brought about through cause-and-effect relationships. We experience karma in the present, based on our past actions, and we accumulate future karma through our actions in the present.

Midheaven—The degree and sign of the zodiac that was in the highest point of the sky at the birth time. The Midheaven is on the ecliptic, and is at the point where the meridian intersects the ecliptic. The meridian is a great circle that intersects the north and south poles, and also is directly overhead at the place of birth.

Modes (or qualities, quadruplicities)—Three ways in which individuals express themselves through their thoughts and actions:

Cardinal—Assertive, ambitious, impatient. The cardinal signs are Aries, Cancer, Libra, and Capricorn.

Fixed—Stable, consistent, patient. The fixed signs are Taurus, Leo, Scorpio, and Aquarius.

Mutable (Common)—Adaptable, responsive, restless. The mutable signs are Gemini, Virgo, Sagittarius, and Pisces.

Psychological types—A method developed by Carl Jung to describe four basic ways that people approach life:

Sensation—This function relates to the world primarily through the five senses.

Thinking—The capacity to recognize the purpose or meaning of what we sense.

Intuition—The capacity to project possibilities into the future.

Feeling—The capacity to determine the value of what we perceive.

Retrograde motion—The apparent change in direction of a planet. Retrograde motion, as perceived from the Earth, occurs because of the relative speed of the Earth and other planets, and because of their positions relative to each other.

Rulership—The association of a planet with a specific house or sign.

Saturn (or other planet) Return—The time when a planet has moved forward (transited) in the zodiac to the same degree it held in the birthchart. These times are significant because the planet's energy is most aligned with the individual's energy when it is in that degree.

Synastry—The comparison of two charts in order to determine compatibility in a relationship.

Appendix 1
Astronomical Data

Planet	Satellite	Discovery	Diameter (km)	Revolutionary Period
(Sun)			1,392,000	225,000,000 years
Mercury			4,878	87,969 days
Venus			12,104	224.7 days
Earth			12,750	365.256 days
	Moon		3,476	27d 7h 43m
Mars			6,787	779.9 days
	Phobos	1877	20x23x28	7h 39m 26.6s
	Deimos	1877	10x12x16	30h 21m 15.7s
Jupiter			54,990	11.86 years
	Amalthea	1892	265x140	11h 57m
	Io	1610	3,640	30h 18m
	Europa	1610	3,130	3d 13h 14m

Planet	Satellite	Discovery	Diameter (km)	Revolutionary Period
	Ganymede	1610	5,280	7d 3h 43m
	Callisto	1610	4,840	16d 16h 32m
Saturn			46,190	29.46 years
	Tethys	1684	1,050	1d 21h 18m
	Dione	1684	1,120	2d 17h 41m
	Rhea	1672	1,530	4d 12h 25m
	Titan	1655	5,720	15d 22h 41m
	Iapetus	1671	1,440	79d 7h 56m
Uranus		1781	51,800	84.01 years
	Miranda	1948	400	33h 55m
	Ariel	1851	1,400	2d 12h 29m
	Umbriel	1851	1,000	4d 3h 28m
	Titania	1787	1,800	8d 16h 56m
	Oberon	1787	1,600	13d 11h 7m
Neptune		1846	49,500	164.79 years
	Triton	1846	3,770	5d 21h 3m retrograde
	Nereid	1949	600	359d 21h 9m
Pluto		1930	2,400	247.7 years
	Charon	1978	1,200	6d 9h 17m

Appendix 2
Creating a Birthchart Using Your CD-ROM Program

First you need to install the program. Just remove the CD-ROM from its folder and place it in your computer's CD-ROM drive. Click on the Start menu and then select "Run." In the Run menu dialogue box, type in your corresponding CD-ROM drive followed by the filename SETUP.exe. Typically, the CD-ROM is set up as D:\

D.\SETUP.exe

The install wizard will run and guide you through the rest of the process.

For an alternate method, you can access your CD-ROM drive by clicking on "My Computer" and then the CD-ROM drive (typically D:\). Double-click the SETUP.exe icon.

You will see an introductory splash screen with the name of the program (it flashes on and off very quickly), and then you will see a screen called "Mapping Your Birthchart." This screen is pictured on the following page.

Mapping Your Birthchart is a basic astrology program, designed around the most sophisticated astrology programming available. Cosmic Patterns, in collaboration with Llewellyn Worldwide, has developed this program to provide you with birthcharts (the circle with all the funny glyphs) and also to provide basic interpretations of those charts (eight to ten-page printouts of information about the chart).

Let's discuss the choices you have:

- The Start button is used to create a chart.

- The About button provides information about Llewellyn Worldwide, the publisher of *Mapping Your Birthchart*, and Cosmic Patterns Software, the designer of the program.

- The Quit button allows you to exit from the program.

Creating an Astrology Chart

To use your program, select "Start" from the menu above, then select "New List of Charts (New Session)." If you are returning to the program and want to see the last chart you made, select "Continue with Charts of Previous Session."

Mapping Your Birth Chart

Tropical Placidus
NATAL CHART

Name:

Date: 05/01/2003   May 1, 2003

Time: 11:04:00 AM

Place:

Instructions:
Type the name of the person. As you type, a pull-down list of names saved on file appears. Until you start saving names, none will appear. To read in a name, click on it. Many people like to enter the name in "Last,First" format rather than "First Last" format so that names can be

Lat & Long: 00° N 00' 00"   000° W 00' 00
Time Zone: 0   Hrs   00   Mins   W   est
Daylight Time: N   (No)
   Ex: Smith,Bill. Note: "SMITH" and "Smith" are different.

List of other Entries (click to Select):

| ✳ Zodiac/House | ✳ Save | ✳ Delete | ✳ New Natal | ✓ Done |

This is where you enter your birth information. There are some simple instructions on the right side of the screen, similar to what follows here. Let's make a birthchart for George W. Bush as an example.

- In the Name box, type "George W. Bush" and Enter.
- In the Date box, type "07061946" (for July 6, 1946) and Enter. You will notice that as you enter the date (in mm dd yyyy format), the cursor will skip to the next part of the date field for you.
- In the Time field, type "0726" (the birth time in hh mm ss format), and "A.M." or "P.M.," and then Enter. You probably won't know the birth time down to the second, so use the right arrow key on your keyboard to skip over that part of the date field as you are typing, or type two zeroes. Here again, you will notice that the cursor moves to the next section of the time field for you.

- In the Place box, type "New Haven, CT" (the birth place). As soon as you type the word "New," a list drops down. Look for "New Haven, CT" in this list by clicking repeatedly on the down arrow. You can go back up by clicking on the up arrow. You will see some places you have probably never heard of, but you will come to "New Haven, CT." Select it. The drop-down list disappears, and you see "New Haven" in the Place box. You will also see information filled in the boxes below it: the latitude is 41N18 00, the longitude is 072W55 00, the time zone is 5 hours 0 minutes West, and the Daylight Saving Time box is marked "Y."

- A number of cities are included in the program's atlas. If your city does not automatically come up, you can use a nearby city from the list. You may also look up your birthplace in an atlas to find the latitude and longitude, time zone, and daylight saving time information, and fill in this information. Generally, a city close to the birthplace will have a longitude and latitude close enough for your purposes and will also be in the same time zone. If the time zone information is different, your chart could be off by an hour one way or the other. Depending on the distance your choice is from your actual birthplace, your chart will be slightly different. You can obtain the correct longitude, latitude, and time information from a time table book for astrology. Two atlases are listed in the bibliography at the end of this book.

- The Zodiac/House button allows you to select a different house system. The program automatically selects the tropical zodiac and the Koch house system. Experiment with the other choices to see what changes on the chart wheel. In this program the interpretation will only change if you select the sidereal zodiac.

- Select the "Save" button at the bottom of the screen to save the chart (you can delete it later if you need to).

- Then select the "Done" button. If you forget to save and go directly to the View button, you will get a prompt asking if you want to save the data. In fact, all the way along prompts appear to help you enter the data.

- This is what you see when you have chosen the Done button:

```
George W.Bush English Cosmo Natal                              _ □ ×
File  Reports  Print  Exit
```

The Mapping Your Birth Chart Report for

George W.Bush

July 6, 1946

7:26 AM

New Haven, Connecticut

```
Calculated for:
Time Zone 5 hours West
Latitude: 41 N 18
Longitude: 72 W 55
Tropical Zodiac, Daylight Savings Time observed.


Positions of Planets at Birth:
Sun      position  is  13 deg.   47 min.   of  Cancer
Moon     position  is  16 deg.   42 min.   of  Libra
Mercury  position  is   9 deg.   50 min.   of  Leo
Venus    position  is  21 deg.   30 min.   of  Leo
Mars     position  is   9 deg.   18 min.   of  Virgo
```

- The next screen has the name of the chart you just entered at the upper left, and it also says "Cosmo Natal." You can see Geroge W. Bush's chart information, and when you scroll down, you read the interpretation.

- If you select the word "Wheel" from the report menu, a chart form appears.

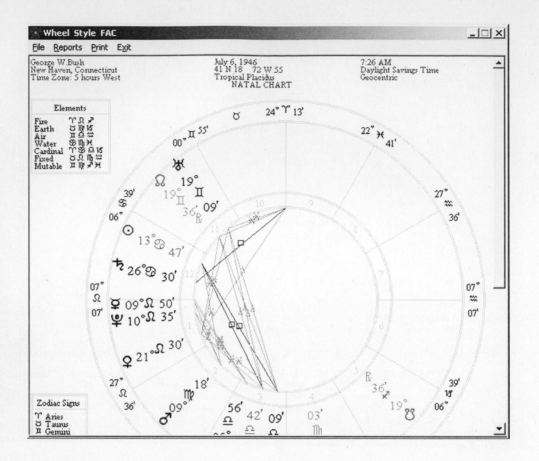

- At the upper left it is labeled "Wheel Style FAC." This form should look just like the one printed here in the book for George W. Bush.

- Select "Print" and then "Print Current Report" to print either the wheel or the interpretation report. Only the item on the screen prints. Select the other option in the Reports menu to change what is on the screen.

- Select "Exit" and then "Yes" to go to the opening screen. From here you can either exit the program, or select "Start" to make another chart and interpretation.

That's it! You can now create charts and interpretations for any birth information you want. This program is so easy to use, you won't need much help. Still, we have included step-by-step instructions for those of you who haven't used an astrology program before.

Bibliography

The American Atlas: U.S. Latitudes and Longitudes, Time Changes and Time Zones. Compiled and programmed by Neil F. Michelson. San Diego, Calif.: ACS Publications, 1978.

Bailey, Alice. *Esoteric Astrology*. New York: Lucis Publishing Co., 1979.

Bennet, E. A. *What Jung Really Said*. New York: Schocken Books, 1967.

Burk, Kevin. *Astrology: Understanding the Birth Chart*. St. Paul, Minn.: Llewellyn Publications, 2001.

Burt, Kathleen. *Archetypes of the Zodiac*. St. Paul, Minn.: Llewellyn Publications, 1999.

Fairfield, Gail. *Choice Centered Astrology*. York Beach, Maine: Weiser, 1998.

Grell, Paul. *Keywords*. Washington: American Federation of Astrologers, 1970.

Holden, James Herschel. *A History of Horoscopic Astrology*. Tempe, Ariz.: American Federation of Astrologers, 1996.

The International Atlas: World Latitudes, Longitudes and Time Changes. Compiled and programmed by Thomas G. Shanks. San Diego, Calif.: ACS Publications, 1985.

Krupp, E. C. *Beyond the Blue Horizon*. New York: Oxford University Press, 1991.

Michelson, Neil. *The American Atlas.* San Diego, Calif.: ACS Publications, 1978, and newer editions.

Monaghan, Patricia. *The New Book of Goddesses & Heroines.* St. Paul, Minn.: Llewellyn Publications, 1997.

New Larousse Encyclopedia of Mythology. Intro. Robert Graves. Trans. Richard Aldington and Delano Ames. New York: Prometheus Press, 1972.

Rudhyar, Dane. *New Mansions for New Men.* Pomona, Calif.: Hunter House, 1978.

Ruperti, Alexander. *Cycles of Becoming.* Davis, Calif.: CRCS Publications, 1978.

Shanks, Thomas. *The International Atlas.* San Diego, Calif.: ACS Publications, 1985 and newer editions.

Tyl, Noel. *Synthesis and Counseling in Astrology: The Professional Manual.* St. Paul, Minn.: Llewellyn Publications, 1998.

Zain, C. C. *Spiritual Astrology.* Los Angeles: The Church of Light, 1960.

Index

225

ORDER LLEWELLYN BOOKS TODAY!

Llewellyn publishes hundreds of books on your favorite subjects! To get these exciting books, including the ones on the following pages, check your local bookstore or order them directly from Llewellyn.

Order Online:
Visit our website at www.llewellyn.com, select your books, and order them on our secure server.

Order by Phone:
- Call toll-free within the U.S. at 1-877-NEW-WRLD (1-877-639-9753). Call toll-free within Canada at 1-866-NEW-WRLD (1-866-639-9753)
- We accept VISA, MasterCard, and American Express

Order by Mail:
Send the full price of your order (MN residents add 7% sales tax) in U.S. funds, plus postage & handling to:

Llewellyn Worldwide
P.O. Box 64383, Dept. 0-7387-0294-3
St. Paul, MN 55164-0383, U.S.A.

Postage & Handling:
Standard (U.S., Mexico, & Canada). If your order is:
Up to $25.00, add $3.50
$25.01 - $48.99, add $4.00
$49.00 and over, FREE STANDARD SHIPPING
(Continental U.S. orders ship UPS. AK, HI, PR, & P.O. Boxes ship USPS 1st class. Mex. & Can. ship PMB.)

International Orders:
Surface Mail: For orders of $20.00 or less, add $5 plus $1 per item ordered. For orders of $20.01 and over, add $6 plus $1 per item ordered.

Air Mail:
Books: Postage & Handling is equal to the total retail price of all books in the order.
Non-book items: Add $5 for each item.

Orders are processed within 2 business days. Please allow for normal shipping time.
Postage and handling rates subject to change.